THE DANCER
FROM KHIVA

THE DANCER
FROM KHIVA

A memoir

Bibish

Atlantic Books
LONDON

Originally published in 2004 as *Tantzovschitza iz Khivy, ili Istoria prostodushnoy* by Azbooka-Klassika Publishing House.

First published in English in the United States of America and Canada in 2008 by Black Cat, an imprint of Grove/Atlantic Inc.

First published in hardback in Great Britain in 2009 by Atlantic Books, an imprint of Grove Atlantic Ltd.

1 3 5 7 9 10 8 6 4 2

A CIP catalogue record for this book is available from the British Library.

ISBN: 978 1 84354 623 8

Printed in Great Britain by the MPG Books Group

Atlantic Books
An imprint of Grove Atlantic Ltd
Ormond House
26–27 Boswell Street
London
WC1N 3JZ

www.atlantic-books.co.uk

This book is dedicated to my American friend, Linda Harris

THE DANCER
FROM KHIVA

I will tell you my story to unburden my heart a little. I think you will surely read the story of my cursed misery to the end. That is my hope.

I come from the East. Yes, I was born in Uzbekistan, not far from Khiva, in a very religious area with its own harsh, merciless laws and customs, its own strange and vicious ways of looking at life.

There is a legend about how Khiva got its name. An old man wandered through the desert for a long time in search of water, he was very thirsty. And finally he found a well. After quenching his thirst, he exclaimed "Khey, vakh!" in his pleasure. After that a town sprang up round the well, and they called it Khivak, and later they started saying simply Khiva. Much earlier, almost two thousand years before, the ancient state of Khorezm was here.

At one time, before the October Revolution, we had a khanate here, and in Russia they had tsars and emperors. Of course, you know about that. Well, the khan of Khiva had many slaves from many different countries. They all toiled hard for him. One of these slaves was my mother's father, who was brought from Iran as a child.

There is one other thing I would like to say about Khiva: Our former leader, Lenin, had only one single medal, which was given to him by my fellow townsmen of Khiva. Lenin did not have any other medals or orders at all.

Yes, I was born in a small *kishlak,* or village, from where we could glimpse the minarets of Khiva. The dreadful thing, as I have said, is that the people there were terribly religious. They observed the laws very strictly, and there was slander and rumor on every side.

My mother's father was known as Kurban-kul, which means "the slave Kurban." He served the khan right up until the revolution. He looked after the camels and fed them. He was a camelherd. When the October Revolution happened in 1917, the Red Army liberated the slaves. But my grandfather could not go back to his homeland in Iran, so he stayed in the village and married a Uzbek woman, my grandmother. They had a little girl, my mother, and another seven brothers and sisters. My mother grew up, and when she was eighteen, she married my father.

You would probably like to know why I am called Bibish. My full name is Hadjarbibi. Hadjar is from the word *hadj,* a pilgrimage. Every devout Muslim, if he is able, must make at least one pilgrimage to Mecca or Medina.

My father's grandfather was called Iskhak Okhun, he studied in a *madrassa* and was the *imam* of the kishlak. And Okhun's father was the secretary of the khan of Khiva. Okhun walked all the way to Mecca to make his hadj. When he came back, he was considered the most pious man in the village. And he told my father, who was only a little boy then:

"My grandson, when you marry and you have a girl-child, name her in honor of my pilgrimage, and let her be as holy as the hadj."

And so I was born Hadjar. And *bibi* means a woman. Together they made the name Hadjarbibi. But when I was a child I was called Hadjar most of the time. Then when my future mother-in-law saw me for the first time, she said: "What a long name—Hadjarbibi. It will take a hundred years to say that. Let's call you simply Bibish!" And so I became Bibish to everyone.

My mother had nine children. In a single year, 1978, two of my brothers and my sister died of different illnesses. And so there were six of us left in the family. One of the boys who died was twelve years old, the girl was two years old, and my youngest brother was only seven days old. I feel so sorry for them.

We lived a very poor life. My father was a teacher in the local village school. My mother didn't have a job anywhere.

She only picked cotton in the collective farm during the season.

My mother was very beautiful, her braids were very long, right down to her heels, thick and black. I remember her face, with smooth skin that glowed. All her neighbors and friends used to ask what her secret was. And I remember our father used to take us into the town on his bicycle (all our father had was a bicycle that was put together out of parts from other bicycles). In the bazaar my father used to buy us apples and melons that were almost rotten. Now I understand why he did that—there was never enough money to feed us.

In the place where we lived, if you pushed a stick into the ground, it would blossom and give fruit. But the problem was that, apart from the school where he taught Russian and Arabic, the only thing my father did was read books. Apart from books, nothing interested him. And it's still the same now. Now he reads not just with glasses, but with a magnifying glass too. And so nothing ever grew in our garden but rushes and grass.

Now I will tell you about the most painful thing that happened in my life. Almost thirty years have passed since that day, and all those years I have kept the memory to myself. I have never shared it with anyone: I was afraid to tell anyone about it.

One summer (I was eight years old then) I asked my mother if I could go to see my grandmother and spend a few days with her. My mother said I could. So I set off. Grandmother lived more than three kilometers away from us. We always walked when we went to see her. I would go on my own, or with one of my brothers, sometimes we walked there with our parents.

So I went out on to the road. And I walked. It was summer, and hot. If you've ever been to our parts, then you know what the heat is like there. Sometimes the temperature reaches forty or forty-five degrees.

Like my mother, I had long, thick braids right down to my heels. And I was plump too. Everyone in the kishlak envied me for having such long braids. My mother always looked after my hair: she used to wash it with the whey from buttermilk and comb it.

And so I walked along. I hardly met anyone at all on the road. One or two people went by with donkeys, that was all. Then I looked back and saw a huge car, probably a jeep, in the distance, coming toward me. The car stopped. A man jumped out, and just like that, he grabbed me and threw me into the car. Two more men were sitting in the car. I began to cry. Then one of then shouted:

"Shut up, or you'll get it!"

I was frightened and I cried quietly, without making any sound. My heart was pounding so hard! The car was moving very fast. One of the men kept hugging me all the time, squeezing me against him, and saying:

"Would you believe it, she still smells of milk. We're lucky, she's fresh, a gift from heaven!"

We drove for a long time and went far into the desert. All I could see all around was desert. It was already afternoon. The driver stopped the car a very long way from the highway. There were thin, prickly bushes growing where the car stopped.

They left me beside the car and walked off to one side. They argued with each other about something for a long time. They shouted and swore. I didn't understand anything they were saying. Then they sat down and smoked something. And then they began laughing like madmen.

I was so frightened I didn't know what to do. So I decided to run wherever my feet took me. I didn't know where I was running to, my head was completely empty. They dashed after me, caught me, and started beating me. They started strangling me with my braids and shouting:

"Where are you running? You're shivering! Are you cold, then? Come to me! You can shout here, no one will hear you!"

They beat me badly, then one of them held my hands in his hand and wound my hair onto his free hand and pulled me toward him, so I couldn't break free. Another one began tearing off my dress and the trousers we wear in our parts, which are called *bakakly-ishtan*. I started crying loudly—it hurt a lot when he pulled me toward him with my hair wound round his hand. The pain was terrible.

One said:

"Look, she hasn't even got any tits!"

Another said:

"Come on, get on with it, we're wasting time."

"What if she doesn't survive?"

"You let me do it, then. And don't worry. If she doesn't survive, the desert's a big place. We'll set fire to her and bury her. Come on, if you don't want to do it, move aside!"

Then one of them fell on me as hard as he could, and I passed out. What they did to me is known only to God. They tormented me so viciously, there are no words to describe it. They raped me mercilessly.

Because I didn't move and didn't react, they probably thought I was already dead. They must have been frightened, so they buried me in the sand. Then they drove away.

I don't know why they didn't burn me as they were planning to do. Perhaps they had run out of matches. Perhaps they simply took fright and decided that if they buried me it would be enough. It's hard to say what they were thinking after my "death." They started hurrying and didn't bury me deep in the sand. Praise be to God! But how much time passed while I lay buried in the sand, I don't remember.

The sand was very hot. Probably that's why I came round. At first I couldn't move. The sand made my eyes itch, my mouth was full of sand. I barely managed to drag myself out. I was very thirsty. All I wanted was to drink. I had terrible pains all over my body from the abuse and the beatings.

I saw my torn panties still lying in the sand. Then I walked in the scorching sun. The sand flies and gadflies bit me all over.

And at night it was very frightening. The snakes and lizards come creeping out at night. There's nothing more terrible in deserts at night than poisonous snakes and lizards! And I had enough sores of my own without them: swellings from the insect bites covered my whole body.

I kept coming round and passing out again. I was so terrified I hardly opened my eyes. I never stopped crying and calling for help, but no one heard me.

All day long I was tortured by the heat and longed for water. But where could I get water? When night came, I was tired, I lay down, looked at the sky, counted the stars, and fell asleep. And even in my sleep the only thing I thought about was water. Although I felt very hungry as well.

In the morning I tried to stand up, but I couldn't, because I wasn't strong enough. When I got up, I fell down, I couldn't keep my balance. So I just lay there. Where could I move to anyway? There was no shade anywhere around. There was nowhere to take shelter. Naked desert all around . . .

In the afternoon a flock of sheep passed close by the place where I was lying. Suddenly I felt someone opening my eyes with his fingers. I looked and saw an old shepherd standing over me and looking to see if I was dead or alive. He tried to get me up, but I kept falling down. I felt very ashamed that I didn't have any panties. I pulled my dress tight round my legs and cried miserably. Finally he got me up, then gave me his stick. He supported me with one hand and began dragging me like that. And we walked for a long time, because I kept falling down. I didn't have the strength to walk.

He took me to his rough shelter made of branches and gave me water from a jug—by then I thought I was going to die any moment without water. It was warm, but it was still water.

Then he washed the sand off my head with the water. I was a terrifying sight. The sores from the insect bites on my arms and legs had festered and they were very painful. At night I kept getting up all the time and drinking warm water. Then I sank back into delirious sleep. I probably had a high fever, because my entire body was shuddering with cramps.

I didn't know how many days I spent with the shepherd, and I still don't know now. After all, almost thirty years have gone by. And how can you count time in the desert? I remember I was very hungry. And what food can a shepherd have in the middle of the desert? Flatbread cakes are the only food I remember. But after so much suffering and hunger, even coarse bread tasted good to me.

Every day I squeezed the pus out of my sores. To this day I still have big scars on my arms. They remind me of this story.

I stayed with the old man in his rough shepherd's shelter. I remember he had a radio and sometimes it used to play music. I thought there was nothing else in the world except this desert, the shepherd, and me.

Before I'd even recovered from one terrible disaster, there was another. Soon the shepherd began pestering me.

"Don't be afraid, I won't touch you, you just stroke it with your hands."

You understand what he was asking me to do.

I began to cry, and he shouted at me:

"You've been with men, what difference does it make to you? You're not a virgin anymore! If I hadn't happened to pass by with my herd, you'd have died, and the wild beasts would have eaten you ages ago! I'm not asking you for much, just stroke it, that's all, and I'll be satisfied. And stop crying, I'm sick of it. Always crying, when there's nothing to cry about! Those things that happened are all over now. Be grateful that I saved you!"

One day the shepherd took his flock a long way away. I'd already decided to run away before that, and so I did. I set out to look for a road to the highway. It was hard for me to find that road in the middle of the desert. If only you knew how I suffered because I didn't have any panties! Just imagine how bad I felt without them and my trousers. And my dress was very dirty and torn. I had to go just as I was.

I finally found the highway, but I was afraid. I felt ashamed to go out on it. And so in the afternoon I lay down beside a prickly bush, and when evening came, I set off along the high-way, walking through the sand. I was walking barefoot, and the sand was hot, it was blistering hot under my feet. I walked a little bit, then rested a little bit. That was how I walked. It was a good thing I'd taken some water with me in a bottle. I drank the warm water one mouthful at a time, very sparingly. But even so it was soon finished.

On my way I saw all kinds of snakes and lizards. I couldn't sleep because of them. And at night it was so quiet, and the stars were so clear and beautiful! There was just a light breeze blowing. Of course, I felt thirsty and hungry again. And my feet were hurt badly by the prickles and the heat—my heels were cracked all over.

Finally one night (the snakes hadn't touched me!) I came to a kishlak. I saw a well beside the first house and lowered the bucket into it, but it got so full I couldn't lift it back up. It was too heavy for me. So I dropped it into the well. And I didn't get a drink of water after all. But I was so thirsty! I walked round the kishlak for a little while and found an *aryk,* a small irrigation ditch, with cloudy, muddy water. So I drank some water from the aryk. What else could I do? At least I quenched my thirst. But after that my stomach started gurgling because there was nothing in it except dirty water.

I slept until morning near someone's house beside a garden.

In the morning I got up and walked round the houses. I knocked at the gates and begged. I asked people to give me something to eat. Some of them gave me a lump of sugar, and some gave me a few bread cakes. Others wouldn't even let me in. They said:

"Go away, we can't even feed our own family!"

Many of them gave me fruit. There's plenty of fruit in our parts. And so I ate my fill and was satisfied for the whole day. The people there probably thought I was a Tajaki gypsy, whole families of whom wander around begging. They're everywhere, in Russia and in Uzbekistan, and now everywhere in the Commonwealth of Independent States too. That's their tradition—to live by begging.

Then I saw some children playing beside their house. I saw them, and I started to cry. It was already late, but it was summer, so it was still light. I stood on the asphalt and cried, and the children called me Baba-Yaga, like the witch in the fairy tale, because I was very dirty. Then some people came up to me and started asking where I was from, who my parents were, where I lived. And I told them I'd got lost.

I remember someone there even felt sorry for me:

"Give her a wash and some clothes and she'd be a normal little girl."

They decided to send me home. They found a man with a motorbike and asked him to take me. Of course, they questioned me first. But I didn't know the name of the collective farm where my kishlak was. I knew there were lakes somewhere nearby, but that was all. Then they asked me what people called my father. I said, "Teacher."

And finally he took me home. I slept all the way in the sidecar of the motorbike, because I was exhausted.

Before my parents could come out into the street, the man who brought me had driven away. My parents were surprised at my strange appearance. My nails had grown as long as the fairy-tale ogré Kashchei the Immortal, and I looked as ugly and dirty as the witch Baba-Yaga. My hair was standing straight up, because I hadn't combed it. Why would a shepherd have a comb if he didn't have a single hair on his head and he walked around stooped over, barely shuffling his feet like a half-dead sheep?

I lied to my parents and said I'd been looking after my grandmother's herd of cows and had no time to take care of myself: I was too lazy. To be honest, most children in our parts run around barefoot and are pretty dirty. In fact that's putting it mildly. People who have a bath or a shower get washed. But those who don't take a bucket of water and pour it over themselves. And that's all. Some people have a primitive sort of washbasin. But for getting washed you can even use a jug. There are all sorts of ways. But if you bathe in the canal or the lakes, you still won't get clean, because the water in them has clay in it, you see. And how could anything be clean round there? Anyway, the way I looked didn't really shock everybody. So my parents never knew, they didn't guess what had happened to me, and I didn't say anything.

But afterward I had to say good-bye to my braids. My head had started to itch back there in the desert, in the shepherd's rough shelter, but now the lice climbed out where they could be seen. I scratched my head for days and nights at a time, until the skin was bloody and raw. In the end my father cut all my hair off. I was sorry to part with my long braids. But on the other hand it was good I didn't have it anymore, because I remembered how one of the cruel brutes in the desert had wound my hair round his hand and pulled it and strangled me with it and how horrible it was and how afraid I was and how much it hurt. When I remembered that, I didn't want to wear a braid anymore. Thank God they didn't burn me and I was still alive. If they'd burned me, I'd be dead now. When I think about that, I shudder all over and I feel really terrible.

You'd probably be interested to know more about my family.

I'll start with my grandfather, an unusual man, and then tell you about my father. His life was a hard one too.

That's what this part of my tale is called:

The Story of My Family

My father's father was called Siddik-makhsum, or Mullah Siddik. People used to come to him from different villages for help. He prayed for people, wrote them various spells against the evil eye and hexes, reconciled husbands and wives, and even wrote a book on magic (decades later the whole family quarreled and fell out because of that book). And he also cured women of infertility. The husbands themselves used to bring their wives to him and leave them there for a few days. My grandfather had a pair of our traditional women's trousers hanging in his doorway. When a woman went in, he used to say to her: "Quick, take your trousers off!" If the woman protested, he used to send her home with the words: "I told you to take your trousers off in the doorway!" But others stayed, and afterward almost all of them got pregnant. Just how did he cure them? Well, it was a great misfortune to remain barren. And afterward there were a lot of little children who looked like my grandfather running around in the kishlaks nearby.

At that time religion was forbidden, the churches and mosques were closed. But people still wanted to believe, and they found people in their kishlaks who carried on preaching and performing the rites in spite of everything.

One night they came to arrest my grandfather in his own home. They arrested and exiled him. He was sent to Siberia for ten years. My father, Nizomiddin, was only three then. My grandmother, Niyazdjan, was left on her own with five children. And that was a terrible, hungry time—the nineteen thirties.

A woman can't manage alone. Niyazdjan went to live with Sadulla, her exiled husband's brother. Sadulla had eight children of his own. Now things were even harder for him. Sadulla provided for the entire family on his own. He was a barber, and he also circumcised boys. He had special instruments for that: a sharpened cane split at the end and a folding razor (my husband told me about them—after all, women aren't allowed at circumcisions!).

In our parts boys are circumcised when they're three to five years old. Circumcisions used to be done at home. The boys were laid on the floor, special beautiful cushions made of satin were put under their legs, their arms were held, and everybody distracted them by showing them money, toys, and presents. And their knees were covered with a towel, so they wouldn't see what was happening. The little bit of skin was squeezed in the slit in the cane and sliced off—whoosh—with the razor. The boys had no time even to realize what had happened. Then they were congratulated, because now they were real men, and given money and presents, and the next day they were already running around outside.

Uncle Sadulla wasn't poor, but he was mean. He locked the food away in the pantry and fastened the key to the belt of his trousers with a pin. Even at night he was never parted from the key. He fed his own family well, but he gave my grand-mother Niyazdjan hardly any food for her children. Two of the children starved to death. Nizom—that was the short form of my father's name—used to cry all the time.

Then one day Niyazdjan stole some bread cakes made with black flour, slit open her mattress and hid the bread there and then fed her children at night. But Sadulla noticed, he took the bread cakes away, and beat her in front of everybody.

As he beat her, Sadulla shouted loudly:

"Do you think it's easy for me to feed my children and yours! I took you in for the sake of my brother Siddik, and you steal from me!"

In the East a woman has no right to contradict a man. Niyazdjan stood there hanging her head, putting up with everything and crying quietly.

Sadulla wanted to marry her off, because she was only twenty-three. At first Niyazdjan couldn't bear the idea, but then she realized she had to save the children and she agreed. She wanted to tell her husband about her misfortune, but how? She couldn't read or write.

Soon they found a bridegroom for her, put her in a cart harnessed to an ass, and took her and her children to a differ-ent family. The sun was terribly hot, and Niyazdjan was sti-fling under her *yashmak*. By the way—women in the East often used to fall ill because they never saw the sunlight!

Sadulla was glad he'd got rid of his burden. The bride price he received for Niyazdjan was fifteen kilograms of grain. And that was all. As far as he was concerned, all my grandmother was worth was fifteen kilograms of grain.

The new husband wanted to have a child of his own, but for a long time my grandmother wouldn't agree. She was afraid of what would happen to her own children. But she had no way out: if a woman doesn't give birth in a year, eastern men take another wife. And the children from a previous marriage don't count.

Soon Niyazdjan had a son. Her husband was very happy. It was his first child, and it was a son as well!

Now it became very difficult for Niyazdjan to manage with the children, and her husband went to her parents' house to fetch her nine-year-old sister Oidin to help.

And this is what happened after that.

One day Niyazdjan was busy with the housework, and she asked her sister to go into the next room and take down the meat hanging on a hook in the ceiling. That was the way they used to keep meat before. There was a pile of bedding and some kind of bundle lying on the floor under the hook. Oidin stood on it to reach the hook. She felt something soft under her feet and then heard a gentle squeal. She felt frightened and went running to fetch her older sister. The new baby was lying on the bedding, wrapped in a robe. When Niyazdjan unwrapped him, the child was already dead . . .

The husband threw Niyazdjan and her children out into the street, and they had to go back to Sadulla. When he saw the exhausted, hungry children, he reluctantly took them in.

A few years later Siddik came back from exile. When he learned his wife had been married to someone else, he renounced her thrice and said: "You are not my wife!" But for the sake of the children he allowed her to stay at his brother's house.

My grandfather gradually became a respected man again. I remember when I was six a wedding was celebrated in our kishlak. A lot of people gathered for it. I was playing with the other children outside in the yard. Suddenly everybody stopped talking. I looked round and saw my grandfather escorted by four other men, two walking in front of him and two walking behind. When the men there saw Siddik-makhsum they stood up, put their hands on their hearts, and bowed their heads. The women who were at the wedding covered their faces with their shawls and went inside into the room, although veils had been abolished a long time earlier.

But let's go back a little bit. In our village there was a cunning woman with no husband who lived with her lame fourteen-year-old niece. When Siddik came back from exile, this woman suggested he could live in her house, and she soon married him to her niece.

My grandfather became a rich man again. He married people, buried them, read prayers at the festival of Ramadan. For this people gave him sheep and fruit. Soon children were born, one after another, to his lame wife.

Niyazdjan and Nizom used to go to help the new wife. Niyazdjan massaged her sick legs. They weren't jealous of each other. Niyazdjan composed verses in honor of her former husband and sang them herself. She taught my father to love his half brothers. And Siddik used to give fruit to her and her son, who still lived with Sadulla.

My father grew up and graduated from secondary school and was glad when he left Sadulla's house to join the army. He served in Saratov and then in Novosibirsk.

One day when he was on leave he met a Russian girl, Anya. They began seeing each other, and they fell in love. Then one day Anya didn't turn up for a date. It was a very cold winter. Nizom waited and waited and finally went to Anya's house. It was the first time he'd ever been to her home, he was very nervous.

He went up to the fourth floor and rang the bell. A woman opened the door and asked in an unfriendly voice:

"What do you want?"

Nizom was flustered and he said the first thing that came into his head:

"Can I have a drink of water?"

"Is there no water in your unit, then?" the woman asked, but she still brought him a huge mug of ice-cold water. And he was already chilled to the bone! But he drank it slowly, hoping that Anya might come out. But she still didn't show up. After that ice-cold water he fell ill. Anya used to visit him. She reminded him about the icy water and they laughed.

When Nizom was demobilized, he went to the telephone exchange where Anya worked and tried to persuade her to marry him, so they could go away together. But the girl refused: her parents were against it, they didn't want their daughter to marry a non-Russian.

When the day for him to go away arrived, Anya came to the train, threw herself into Nizom's arms, and said she was pregnant. Nizom almost went out of his mind. But what could he do? How could he stay in Novosibirsk, when his mother was living alone in poverty and Anya's parents wouldn't let her marry him?

It was a very painful parting. They stood on the platform and cried with their arms round each other. Later my father learned that soon afterward Anya had a miscarriage.

When he came back from the army, my father graduated from the pedagogical institute in Urganch and began teaching Uzbeki language and literature. And then Niyazdjan decided to marry her son off. But it is very hard to find a bride when you're poor, and Niyazdjan was also refused because her husband had left her and married another woman.

Siddik's neighbors and relatives criticized Siddik for not worrying about his son's future. And then Siddik began looking for a bride for my father. As he was riding round the kishlak, he met Kurban-kul on the road. Kurban-kul bowed respectfully to Siddik-makhsum, and they began talking. And so Siddik found out that Kurban had a daughter, and they agreed to make a match.

When he got home, Siddik told everyone the good news.

My father was terribly anxious: "What's she like? What does she look like? Is she ugly?" You see, in our parts the bride-groom and the bride can't see each other before the wedding. Nizom wouldn't accept this custom. He found out where his bride-to-be lived and set out to take a look at her in secret.

Not far from the house he climbed up an old mulberry tree and began to wait. He sat there the whole day without seeing anything. Finally he saw a girl walking along, driving cows back from pasture. And she was going straight toward the house where his bride lived. My father could see only the girl's back. Then he whistled quietly, hoping she would turn round. And she did turn round! My father jumped down from the tree, and there he was facing a pretty girl with a round face and big black eyes. And her eyebrows were like swallow's wings. The girl took fright and ran off into the house in a flash.

Nizom went back home as if nothing had happened, and as he went to bed the only thing he could think of was his bride.

Finally the matchmakers were sent to call and the day of the wedding was set. Only at the wedding did Asila learn that the young man who had tumbled down out of the tree was her future husband.

After the wedding the newlyweds lived with Uncle Sadulla, and then Siddik built a house for them, and men from all over the kishlak came to help with it.

Houses used to be built without foundations, and so they didn't last long. But in those clay houses it was cool in summer and warm in winter. My parents moved into the new house with my grandmother Niyazdjan.

It was four years before my mother had her first child, a son. And two years after that I was born.

My grandmother wrote her verses and sang them while she played the mandolin. First she would ask a guest what his name was, then immediately she would compose a poem in his honor and sing it. At all the weddings and festivals she sang and danced with the other women and played the mandolin.

And still she went to my grandfather Siddik's house to help his lame, sick wife, who had borne eight children.

Beside his house, my grandfather Siddik had a big pool and that was his special place for resting. He used to lie on his side, propped up with one elbow on a cushion, drinking green tea from a bowl and smoking a hookah. When he drew in the smoke, you could hear the water gurgling in the hookah, and the smell of fragrant tobacco spread all around. But my grandmother Niyazdjan sat in the house with my grandfather's wife, treating her legs with all sorts of herbs. Later the lame woman's children grew up, and became literate people, they knew Arabic. But she died of grief after the death of her youngest daughter from appendicitis—when the ambulance arrived it was already too late for them to save the girl.

*   *   *

As I've already said, we lived a poor life. My father was the only one who had a job. Only one of our rooms had a floor and a real divan in it. My mother kept that room locked. It was for guests. Our ceilings were made out of reeds. When the roof leaked, my father used to take some straw, mix it with clay, and patch the roof like that. The well was outside, and so was the toilet. And my mother used to cook on a *tandyr*, a special stove made of scorched clay that she heated with the dry plants left over after the cotton was picked. But there weren't enough of these plants, and every time my father had a vacation from the school he went away into the sands for a few days to gather firewood for the winter. He used to hire a tractor driver with a trailer to bring back dry saxaul, the only kind of tree that grows in the desert.

We all slept in one room. My mother used to spread out a felt mat of sheep's wool on the floor and put mattresses on the mat. And then we went to bed. There were a lot of fleas in the felt mat. During the night we used to scratch ourselves and cry. Our mother used to switch on the light and drive away the fleas. After a while the felt mat was changed for a carpet.

Our mother put us in the kindergarten at the collective farm, and she raised silkworms at home. She fed the larvae fresh mulberry leaves. Soon the worms turned into cocoons, and they were quickly gathered up and handed in at special collection points.

*   *   *

One day, when I was five—in the summer, in the heat—this is what happened. We always kept water for washing our hands outside in a *kumgan* (that's what the special jug is called). I went outside to play dolls with the other girls. I used to make the dolls out of sticks. I tied strings to a stick and dressed the stick in a rag, and we made all the rest ourselves out of clay. I was sitting there playing, and I felt thirsty. I looked and saw the kumgan standing there and I went across and picked up the kumgan and started gulping down water—and I almost swallowed a bumble bee! It had enough time to sting me on the tongue. How I screamed at the pain! I spat the bumble bee out, it fell on the ground and started crawling away slowly, it must have got soaking wet in the kumgan. A few minutes later my tongue swelled so much that I almost choked. My parents were frightened, and they called an old medicine woman. She smeared my tongue with clay. Then it was easier to breathe.

Sometimes I used to think it would have been better for me to die then, when I was five, so that I wouldn't suffer anymore . . .

When I turned seven, the director of the school came to our house and said to my father:

"Nizom, if you like, I'll take your daughter to the young pioneer camp, she can have a little vacation before school, you know my children are at the camp too."

"All right, I'll just call her," my father said, and he asked me, "Well, daughter, will you go to camp?"

I was very curious to see what camp was like—I didn't have any idea, because I wasn't going to school yet. My father said:

"Go and get dressed. He'll come to collect you in a minute."

My mother wasn't home. I went to the cupboard, found all my warm things, and put everything on: several pairs of trousers, two or three pairs of socks, a jumper, a pullover. I was afraid it would be cold in the camp. I thought it was a long way away from us and I'd be freezing! But it was forty degrees outside. I went out into the street, and the director of the school was standing there with his motorbike. Neither the director nor my father looked at how I was dressed. And the director drove me away.

The camp was on our collective farm, not very far away from our house. We lived in brigade number five, and the camp was in brigade number one. And I thought we were going a long way away, where it would be cold, so I'd put on all the winter clothes I had. At least I hadn't put my coat on, although I should have (that's a joke). By the time we reached the camp, I sweated so much in the heat it felt like I was taking a hot bath. The sweat was streaming off me.

An old man, the property manager, came out of a room and said to me:

"Let's go, I'll give you a form."

We went into the storehouse. He gave me a form and said:

"There, get changed and put your things over there, separately, then I'll take them and write your name on them. When you come back at the end of the camp session, you can put your things on again. Hurry up now, the kids will be back from their hike any minute, you're going to have lunch."

I was left on my own in the storehouse. And there was no way I could take my clothes off, because everything I was wearing was soaked with sweat. I struggled for a very long time and the old man must have started to worry why I was taking so long. When he couldn't wait any longer, he came in to see what I was doing.

"Why haven't you put the uniform on?"

I said:

"I can't get my clothes off."

He sat me down on the floor and began taking my clothes off and saying angrily:

"Thinking of going to Siberia, were you? I said, were you going off to Siberia? Why did you put so many clothes on?" And he scolded me, because he was old and he could barely manage to take off all the things I had on. And I really had thought I was going to Siberia, only the camp turned out to be only walking distance away.

These days I often remember funny stories like that.

In second or third grade the teacher made me class monitor. I'd always wanted to be first, it was a kind of longing I had. I was in the same class as girls who were my neighbors and friends and lived on the same street as me. And we were friends with girls from the other class too, and we used to play with them after school.

One day one of the girls got mad at me because I wouldn't let her copy my homework. When we were on our way home, she turned all the other girls against me. The summer vacation happened to begin just then. When I went out into the street to play with the girls, they ran away and wouldn't talk to me. It went on for a long time, and I was miserable because I was all alone—no one wanted to play with me. I used to stay home all the time. And that girl was glad no one was friends with me.

Finally I couldn't stand it anymore—I was still a child, I wanted to play, to jump and dance and sing. And my mother had two beautiful dresses made of crepe de chine. She always took care of those dresses and wore them only for weddings and birthdays, or when she went into the town, those were the only times she put them on. They were hanging in the cupboard. When my mother was out, I took those dresses, found some scissors, and began cutting them into pieces. The two dresses made quite a lot of pieces, and I threw away all the unnecessary parts—the sleeves and the collars. I took the strips I'd cut and went to the other girls. I gave some to everyone, just as long as they made up with me. Of course when I gave them the beautiful ribbons, we were friends again.

Later I paid a heavy price for that friendship. My mother discovered that her dresses had disappeared from the cupboard and told my father that the girls were wearing bows made of

the same material as her dresses. My father realized what I'd
done right away and he gave me a beating that I still remember even now.

And here is another memory. I was twelve. I was at home,
watching television. There was a wedding at the neighbors'
house, and my parents and brothers had gone out to the wedding. I was going to go later. Suddenly I felt something warm
running down my leg. I took my trousers off and saw blood.
I was so frightened, I thought I was going to die on the spot.
I had no idea where the blood had come from. I ran for my
mother, who was at the wedding at the neighbors' house, and
I told her quickly:

"Mama, mama, I'm going to die now!"

My mother was frightened:

"Don't say things like that, or else they'll come true! What's
happened?" and she took me outside.

"Mama, I'm bleeding, I'm going to die now, aren't I?" I
asked.

My mother got all flustered too.

"Where's the blood, where are you bleeding?"

When we got home, she saw the blood on my trousers and
realized straightaway what was wrong with me. She scolded
me for making such a fuss, took my trousers off, and washed
them with household soap and cold water. Then we made
"liners" for me out of a rag. It turned out to be my first period,

the same as every girl has. But I thought the blood would never stop and I was going to die.

I was a good student at school. At first I used to sit at the front desk, but later I found out that in the desks at the back you could eat bread cakes during class, so I moved. But the bread I had didn't taste very good—until we got a cow, my mother used to bake the cakes with just water. Then I used to let the poor students copy from me, and they gave me tasty bread cakes in return.

And so the years passed, and I grew up a bit. No one at all ever found out about what happened to me in the desert. That accursed story has been preserved only in my memory.

After I finished eighth grade I went to Khiva with my father. I was going to apply to the women's pedagogical institute that trained teachers for elementary school. I was a good student, and so the school accepted me without any exams. I went to live for a while with my grandmother, my mother's mother.

In our parts all girls are supposed to know how to cook before they get married. When my mother tried to make me cook something or help around the house, I always used to run off to play outside. And when she scolded me and said I ought to know how to do everything else as well, that it would come in useful, I wouldn't listen to her. I remember how she used to chase me and beat me with the broom, and one day when I rolled out a bread cake crookedly, she grabbed the rolling pin out of my hands and hit me across the fingers with it. But it was all in vain: I didn't want to do anything around the house. Instead I was always either reading a book or dancing.

And so no one taught me how to cook. My grandmother had four sons, and so she had four daughters-in-law. In our parts, when a daughter-in-law is in the house, everyone else— the sisters-in-law and the granddaughters—takes it easy. So those four daughters-in-law used to feed me. I remember the poor creatures getting up in the morning, cleaning, sweeping, boiling food, watching the cows (there were eight cows) and the chickens. And looking after their husbands. And bringing up their children.

One day those cows got me into a real adventure. One of the daughters-in-law milked the cows twice a day. Early in the morning and late in the evening. After the milking she used to bring a bucket full of milk, which she always hung up in the same place, and which she covered with gauze so that the insects wouldn't get into it.

But I used to get up early in the morning every day, get the bucket down, take off the gauze, stick my fingers into the milk, and then lick them: overnight the cream set really, really thick. Every day I stole the cream out of the bucket. The poor daughter-in-law said:

"Listen, the cows' milk used to be good, but just recently I simply can't churn the butter, it doesn't work. Maybe they need different feed? I don't know what to do."

But the other daughters-in-law said:

"Oh no, the feed's all right, the grass is fine, we feed them on time, we clean up on time. Maybe the cows are ill?"

Nobody ever suspected that it was me stealing the very tastiest morsel until one of my uncles discovered me when he came out to the toilet. He gave me a good beating and then said:

"Don't do that again, we have mouths as well, and we want to eat too!"

Those words taught me a lesson for the rest of my life.

During breakfast, lunch, and dinner, my grandmother had the habit of watching your mouth. It used to annoy me. Now when someone's sitting beside me and eating—guests or anyone else—I never watch their mouths: let them eat as much as they want.

My hair had grown right down to my knees again. Once again everyone admired my cursed braid, the cause of all my misfortunes! No one else in the college had such a long braid.

Like the other girls, I had developed breasts. I was pretty well completely grown up.

I finished the first year with good grades. I was glad that at least now I'd get a scholarship. Of course, that was a wonderful thing for any student. Who would have thought the tragedy that happened in my childhood could be repeated?

Now I'll tell you about that as well.

One day in summer—yes, it was summer again—I was walking home after my exams. A car stopped on the road. Not a big one, like that time, but a small saloon, a white Zhiguli, a Soviet car. There were three men sitting in it this time too. They called out to me:

"Hey miss, can we give you a lift? Where are you going? Get in, we'll give you a lift."

One of them got out and began trying to persuade me to get into the car. I refused without even turning round and walked on along a path—after all, the car couldn't drive along that. There were mulberry trees growing there, that was why I went that way. But he ran after me, grabbed me in his arms, easily dragged me back to the car, and pushed me into the backseat. And this happened in broad daylight, quite close to the town. The three men were about twenty-one, twenty-nine, and thirty-three, I think. I didn't know those first ones. But I know these. They're probably still alive now.

The car set off. They took me to some kind of warehouse. They led me out of the car and pushed me in the back to drive me into a room where there was nothing but a bed. It was probably the watchman's room, I don't know.

The first to come in was the young one, who was twenty or twenty-one, and the other two waited outside in the yard. And then he began undressing me. I tried to defend myself, I resisted and cried and pushed him away from me, I told him I was a virgin. And he answered:

"Good, all right, if you really are a virgin, I'll marry you, but if you cheat me, then expect no mercy. Let's find out," and he threw himself on me.

He raped me viciously, and of course there was no blood. I couldn't tell him that when I was eight years old I'd been raped in the desert. And then he began to beat me wherever he could, he kicked me and battered me with his fists. And on his way out, he said:

"That's for lying to me, you rotten bitch, there, take that!" and he kicked me again and again in the stomach.

They hadn't taken pity on me when I was only a child of eight, they'd buried me alive, so why would they take pity on me this time? They didn't. They treated me the same way. They stood in line too.

The second one came in and punched me in the head. He bit me all over my body with his foul teeth, did what he wanted and went out.

Then the third one appeared. I had no strength left at all. I was almost fainting. When I opened my eyes and saw this third one, I flung myself off the bed on to the floor and crawled toward him on my knees, sobbing and begging him not to touch me. He didn't come near me. He just came in and stood there. I crawled toward him. The other two had already gone away. And then this last one said to me:

"You can't report us, because even before us you weren't a virgin, and then everyone will find out. So think about it. If you want to live, keep quiet. You understand?"

I nodded.

He drove me home and then spread the rumor in the kishlak that I wasn't a virgin. Of course I was shattered. Just like the first time, I didn't say a word, I didn't tell anyone anything, I kept everything inside. It was the second time the name Hadjar—pilgrim—had failed to save me.

After that day I started thinking—kill them! After all, I knew them! The others, who had maimed me in the desert, I hadn't known them. And even if I had, what could I have done then, a child of eight! But this time I knew all three men. I remember the youngest wasn't married, and another worked in the militia.

First I wanted to burn down one of their houses. I worked out a plan. But nothing came of it, or rather, I wasn't brave enough. Then I thought it would be good to go to law college and become a prosecutor and try them myself. Day and night I wondered what I ought to do, what I could do. I racked my brains over it all the time. Sometimes I even wanted to die. Simply die and nothing else.

When I was very little, my grandmother Niyazdjan once told me a legend.

Here it is:

THE LEGEND OF THE CURSE

One day God ordered all the people to bring him one chicken egg each. The people were surprised—what was it for? But they did as God ordered. And all the eggs piled up into an entire mountain.

Then God said:

"And now take one egg each."

People did as God said, but they asked:

"We don't understand, what does this mean?"

God answered:

"If anyone got back the same egg he put in, he will receive a gift: anyone who offends that person or causes him grief will be cursed. And this gift will be passed on from generation to generation."

"But how do we know who took his own egg and who took someone else's, when all eggs look alike?"

"Yes, but I know," God told the people.

I asked my grandmother at the time:

"And the man our family is descended from, which egg did he take?"

She said:

"When the time comes, you'll understand that for yourself."

I remembered this legend when the mother of one of the men who attacked me died suddenly and another was badly hurt when he crashed his car with all his family in it.

But then, perhaps it was simply a coincidence? I don't know . . .

I was a good student at the pedagogical college. I spent time in the library, acted in drama clubs, took part in sporting contests and district competitions . . . And I danced in a folk music ensemble at college as well. By the way, in the kishlaks in our parts they don't like girls like me. They think dancing is disgraceful. It's shameful.

And then one day they showed me on regional television. I was dancing with the ensemble. You know, I'd always danced, ever since I was a child!

But early in the morning the rumors had started. The whole village had seen me on television. After that concert I couldn't hold my head up in public anymore, neither could my relatives or my parents. Some people even shouted at me in the street:

"There goes the dancer. It's disgraceful, you've brought shame on all of us! There were never any clowns in our village before, you're the first!"

They spread the rumor that I'd abandoned my studies and become a dancer. But despite everything, I carried on living the way I thought was right. Even though I knew it would turn out badly. One day I even managed to get into a crowd scene at the Kazakhfilm studios. The film was called *The Legend of Chokan*. I remember they paid us after the film— five Lenin roubles each.

It was easy to see me in the shot, with my braids. The shot lasted only a few seconds, but even so it was a great success.

And that was when it began: Every time I came home, there would be another row because of me. My brother started beating me for my misdemeanors. And he said:

"You've brought shame on us—first you dance, and then you appear on television! We're sick of you and your stupid tricks!"

I wanted to run away from home and go far, far away, but I had no idea where to go. I was exhausted and depressed all the time, and I began to get pains in my heart. I kept thinking how desperately unlucky I was. At night I couldn't get to sleep, I suffered from terrible insomnia. I danced, and what came of it? Nothing but pain and suffering.

The rape, the rumors—it all weighed down on me. More and more often I wanted to die. And then I remembered that my grandmother Niyazdjan once said to me:

"Never trim your nails in the evening. It's a bad sign. If you're going to trim your nails, do it as far away as possible from the tablecloth where we eat our bread. If a nail gets into your stomach by accident, it will be dreadfully painful because the nail will start to grow there inside you."

She probably really did believe that.

* * *

So one day I decided to die. I trimmed all my nails and drank the trimmings with some water and then, like a fool, I waited to die. I didn't.

Another time I threw myself into the big canal that brings the water from the Amudarya. But that didn't work either. I deliberately sank to the bottom, I didn't swim back up, and I swallowed lots of water. But a man saw me and plunged in to save me. He couldn't keep hold of me because the current was strong. So he grabbed hold of my hair and pulled me out of the water that way. My accursed braid, it wouldn't even let me die in peace!

And some time later I took a whole handful of some medicines and poisoned myself. But I still survived.

After all this stress and suffering I was in the hospital twice, in the neurological department. And I showed the patients there my dances too!

After that someone started a rumor in the village that I was pregnant. And I fell into depression again, I didn't have the strength to struggle. I was still too young—only sixteen!

And then they took me to a graveyard in the Shavat district, where they used to take mentally ill people, children and grown-ups, to pray for help at the grave of Yusuf-Hamadan-pir. People used to come from different districts and regions. They brought meat, rice, and flat cakes of bread, and left them for those who spent the night in the graveyard, in special houses made of clay: separate houses for women and for men.

In the middle of this graveyard, I remember, was a little hill, and women who couldn't have children used to lie on the ground and roll down it and ask God to give them children.

In the evening everyone sat and prayed to be made well. And in the morning they asked what you'd seen in your dreams. And they told me: wait, you're sure to have a dream.

And then at last I did have a dream. I saw an old man with a gray beard. He was wearing a long velvet robe. In one hand he was holding a stick and in the other a white bundle. He put the bundle down beside me and said: "Wake up, daughter, I will reveal your calling to you. You must dance. Here, take your clothes!" And with those words he unwrapped the bundle. There was a dancing costume inside it. And that was all.

I woke up feeling as if it wasn't a dream and I'd really seen the old man. This Muslim saint is called Hazrati Hizr and you have to do everything he says. It's fate. And so that was that.

At about that time there was a rift between the families of the two brothers—Siddik and Sadulla. This is how it happened:

The Story of the Magic Book

The brothers had decided a long time ago to marry their children to each other. In Muslim countries close relatives marry each other—male and female cousins marry. In our parts it's simply thought of as the way of things. When a family wants to marry off a daughter, her father first gathers together his close relatives and says: "Look, they want to betroth my daughter. What do you think, shall I give my daughter in marriage to a stranger, or will one of you take her for his son?" If his brother or sister doesn't want to take her for their son, then they say: "No, my son isn't planning to marry yet." Or they'll say: "Don't give her to strangers. I want to marry my son to your daughter." In any case, relatives and close friends have to be asked. When people want to marry off their sons, they ask their relatives and friends first too.

And so the two brothers had decided to reinforce their family ties, since they themselves were already old. Siddik had an unmarried eldest son and a daughter to give away, Sadulla also had a son and a daughter. Soon afterward Siddik married his son to Sadulla's daughter.

You remember I told you that my grandfather Siddik wrote a book on magic in Arabic. He never let anyone read it. He hid it. Siddik's children knew about this. They all wondered how they could get hold of this book and take possession of the experience and knowledge that were in it. Sadulla's daughter, who was now Siddik's daughter-in-law, knew Arabic too, because when she was a little girl she used to visit her uncle Siddik and his children and so learned Arabic. She wanted to get hold of the book as well. My father was the only one who made no claims. He knew his half brothers and sisters wouldn't give him the book. And he comforted himself by saying: "I don't want anything from my father. I'm grateful to him for finding me a wife and for building us a house."

Soon after this my grandfather Siddik-makhsum died. After the funeral a scandalous argument broke out beside his house over the book. The problem was that Sadulla's daughter had managed to steal the book and hide it, but so far no one knew that she'd stolen it. Siddik's children almost went crazy.

One was shouting:

"Papa was going to give me that book!"

Another said:

"No, he loved me best! If I find the book, it's mine!"

They began searching the entire house. They didn't find it.

But Sadulla's daughter gave herself away somehow. They began to suspect her and they followed her. She realized it was dangerous to keep the book at home. She decided to hide it in her father Sadulla's house. At night she got up and crept out to the cowshed, where she'd hidden the book. But her husband wasn't sleeping, he followed his young wife. When she came out of the cowshed, he seized her by the arm and grabbed the book. He shouted:

"Thief, you have no right to our father's book!"

At the sound of the shout everyone came running and a real fight began. Everyone wanted to have the book. Sadulla's daughter wouldn't give in. She was envious because people called all Siddik's daughters *halifa*. That's a mark of great respect. Girls and women took special lessons with tutors to become a halifa. They were taught to read and write Arabic, they studied customs and traditions. And they also had to have an immaculate voice. Halifas were always in demand, especially at funerals. They were paid lots of money for reading the holy book during the rituals.

People called Siddik's sons *makhsumams*. All my father's half brothers and sisters earned good money and were respected by people.

Sadulla's daughter wanted to be the same as they were. She was obsessed with the dream of being a halifa. When she got her hands on the book again she said furiously:

"May this book never be yours or mine!" and she burned it quickly. After that she was thrown out of the house with her child in her arms.

When he saw his daughter, Sadulla was furious and he told his son:

"Send your wife back to her parents!"

"Why, papa?"

"Because my brother's children have thrown your sister out. So now their sister can leave here!"

"But everything is fine between us, there's a little baby . . ."

"All the same, if you're my son, you must do as I say!"

And so for no reason at all, the poor woman was sent back home with her child. That was how the family ties between the two brothers were destroyed. Forever. And a priceless book was lost.

*　*　*

Our family began living its own life. My older brother had a job. My younger brothers were studying. I fell in love, like all girls. But, alas, it was pointless. I had no chance of getting married. In our parts, if you're not a virgin then there's no question of getting married. Every path was closed to me. If only you knew how much I suffered! Why were there only dark times in my life, where were the bright periods?

I put up with all the attacks at home in those years, just so that I could finish my studies. I went on tour round the district with the folk music ensemble, and I took part in the cotton harvest.

And that's a separate story:

The Story of the Cotton Harvest

I want to tell you about it in detail. Uzbekistan is famous for its cotton.

In summer all the Uzbeki women go out to harvest the cotton, generation after generation.

Students from schools, colleges, and universities used to be sent to harvest the cotton too. They didn't study much, except in winter. Most of the year they were busy in the cotton fields.

From February onward they water the cotton fields. In March they sow the seeds, and when the cotton grows, they weed it by hand. Then they heap the earth up around it with mattocks—they do that by hand too. It's painstaking, heavy work. The weather starts to get very hot. They go out into the fields from early morning until late evening. After they heap up the earth around the cotton, they water it again. And so when they collect the harvest, their feet are always in water, and their heads are in the hot sun.

In June and July the cotton blossoms with beautiful pale yellow flowers. In the middle of August they start topping the shoots: they pull a prickly shoot off the cotton—if it's not torn off, the seed capsule won't form and the cotton will all go into growth. The shoot is very sharp and you get your fingers badly pricked.

Soon the cotton bolls open up one by one and the fields turn snow-white. Then they start gathering the harvest.

My mother used to go out into the cotton fields from morning till night. She took a sack with her and an apron to collect the cotton in. She bent down, gathering the open bolls with both hands. She filled the apron and then tipped it into the sack. They took these sacks to someone called a tableman at a special weighing point. For this slave labor they were paid a pittance. But there was no other work in the kishlak.

When I was studying in the pedagogical institute, they used to send us out to the cotton fields too. The professor used to be very angry if we didn't fulfill the daily norm. But how could we fulfill it, when cotton is so light it hardly weighs anything at all, and everyone was expected to gather eighty or a hundred kilograms a day? The professor's wife had a long, thin switch.

In the evening she used to gather us together in a room and shout:

"Hold your hands out in front of you!"

When we held our hands out, she began beating the fingers of the ones who hadn't fulfilled the daily norm with that switch of hers. And I wasn't interested in fulfilling and over-fulfilling the plan. So I often got beaten on the fingers. And believe me, it really hurt.

Perhaps those "front-rank workers of socialist competition" really did exist. But I think a lot of the time the records were doctored. In Brezhnev's time Uzbekistan's plan was five million tons! Just imagine anyone fulfilling that!

For picking cotton they paid you a few kopecks or they didn't pay at all. Our labor had no value. But the plan always had to be fulfilled. If a brigade, a collective farm, or a district fell behind, then they made them work at night as well. They tied rags round sticks, soaked them in kerosene, and walked round the fields with them so that people could work in the dark. And no one dared to protest. Everyone worked and said nothing. Just like in the days of serfdom.

If anyone didn't show up in the cotton fields and they didn't have a very serious reason, a militiaman would come and make them go.

Sometimes they kept us in the cotton fields until the beginning of December. The fields were already empty, but they wouldn't allow us to go until the order came down from "on top."

And then later I learned that this cotton used to rot in the big warehouses in Russia. All our appalling effort went to waste. Then who needed it? Was it all just so that the bosses in Uzbekistan could report back to the bosses in Moscow, was that it?

That was the way things were.

True, after the cotton harvest, they used to hold big celebrations for the people, they were called *pakhta-bairam*. There was a stadium in Khiva, they used to set up a stage there and bring in all sorts of performers. There were even ram fights, cock fights, and horse racing. The whole republic used to celebrate.

Then my last state exams began, my final days as a student in the college.

One day I was walking along the sidewalk in the college and I saw a group of young men coming toward me.

These young men stopped me and asked:

"Miss, can you tell us where the bazaar is?"

I pointed out the way to them with my finger. I couldn't answer. Because I only knew Russian in theory, only some elementary words from school. I'd never had to use Russian. Because where I lived was just a big backward village! And who could I talk to in Russian, if there were no Russians in our parts? I remember, when they talked to me, I was like a deaf-mute. I could more or less understand them, but I could hardly answer. I spoke hardly any Russian. I just nodded my head, and that was all. But we understood each other all right anyway.

And then they asked me:

"Where's the municipal executive committee?"

I took them there. They turned out to be students from Leningrad. They'd come to Khiva to write about Uzbeki customs and rituals.

They had their professor with them, their supervisor, a Georgian woman called Genriko Sergeevna Kharatishvili. A beautiful woman, educated, cultured, and not at all affected. She told me they had nowhere to spend the night, because Khiva was a museum city, the hotels were almost always full.

I wanted to take them home with me. Only I lived in such a terrible old house, it didn't even have a normal floor or ceiling. I felt ashamed about it. Of course, my father wasn't prosperous. While we were little he worked to support everyone on his own. When we grew up, my brother and I went to college to study. So my father hadn't been able to build a new house.

Then I decided to put them in our student hostel. I took Genriko Sergeevna to the director of the college. The director immediately made time to see them and gave them a room where they could rest and spend the night. I got to know them better. We agreed to meet in the morning so that I could show them the interesting sights of Khiva. I came early the next day, and we set off on foot round the museums and saw everything.

At that time we were having class parties at college. Every Saturday and Sunday the students went round the districts visiting each other. And then one girl student invited us— my guests and the students in her year—to a party. She lived forty kilometers from Khiva.

I paid for them to get there—the Russian students, I mean— out of my thirty-rouble grant. I didn't mind spending money on them. We had a really good time at the party, no one slept. They only fell asleep early in the morning because they were tired. Everyone came back pleased and in a happy mood.

Genriko Sergeevna was happy with our hospitality too. She was really pleased that her students had a good time and enjoyed themselves so much.

A week later they left to go to another town. Of course, I saw them off at the railroad station. Before the train came we sang songs, and they gave me their addresses. They were studying the Afghan language and Arabic at Leningrad State University—they were future orientalists. Two of them were from Germany—Lutz (that's a short form of Ludwig) and Tibor. Giya (that's short for Georgii) was from Leningrad, Victor from Gatchina, Zarina from Kazakhstan, and Svetlana from Gorki, and Oleg was from Kaliningrad. They invited me to visit them in Leningrad. Their invitation gave me strength and made me believe that I would get away from my kishlak somehow.

When they left, I pulled myself together: I had to get out of there as soon as possible. I'd dreamed about it all the time before. Only I hadn't known where to go. But now I knew.

After I graduated from the pedagogical institute, I got my diploma and rushed straight home. When I got here, I told my mother:

"I'm going to go away to Leningrad, I'm not going to stay in this rotten hole any longer, there's nothing here but vicious rumors! I've had enough!"

My mother was frightened:

"Don't do anything stupid, you've caused us enough trouble as it is. Don't go away, daughter, you've got your diploma now, you work in the school with your father, all right?"

It was all pointless. She talked to me and tried to persuade me, but I didn't want to listen to her anymore. I had only one thought in my head—how could I run away? I had to choose a time when my father and brother weren't at home. It was all I could think about.

And then one day I got up early in the morning and saw my father had gone to the school and my older brother had gone to work. After college he found a job in the municipal house of culture as a specialist on teaching methods. And in his free time he played the accordion at weddings as well. My father saved up the money for that accordion.

There was no one at home apart from my mother and me. So now was the best time to run away! I had breakfast and began collecting my summer things. I took out my father's "hundred-years-old" suitcase. But what about money? You can't run very far without money. There was only one place in the house where money was kept—my father's trunk.

I opened the trunk and took out exactly five hundred Lenin roubles. I remember how my heart was trembling in fear. After all, five hundred roubles was a lot of money for a poor man. It was four times my father's monthly pay.

I took six bread cakes for the journey, but on the way to Moscow they turned rock hard, so that it was impossible to eat them. If my father had been at home, I couldn't have opened the trunk, and I wouldn't have taken the five hundred roubles. Then I would probably have stayed at home.

I remember my mother crying and saying:

"What shall I tell your father? And other people?"

I didn't answer, I was in a hurry to get away while my father and brother weren't at home.

I took the bus to Urganch—twenty-five kilometers from our town—and arrived at the railroad station. The train was due any minute, and there weren't any tickets for Moscow. Yes, during the summer, tickets for Moscow were always in short supply. Melons, watermelons, tomatoes, cucumbers, green herbs—you understand, everybody goes to Moscow to sell their fruit and vegetables.

When the train arrived at the station, I agreed on a price of seventy roubles with a conductor, when a ticket to Moscow cost only twenty-two roubles! But there weren't any left in the ticket office.

Three days later I was in Moscow, standing in line for the ticket office at the Leningrad Station. I was terribly tired after the train journey. After all, it was the first time I'd traveled a long way on my own. I spent half an hour getting ready to say two words to the ticket clerk: "Leningrad please." Then my turn came and I got confused. The ticket clerk said:

"Where to? Speak up."

I didn't say anything. She tried to hurry me:

"Come on, speak up, which way are you going, where to?"

"Leningrad please," I said.

She said:

"There are tickets to the Finland Station, will that do?" (This is the name of the station, which I didn't know.)

"I don't want Finland!" I said, frightened.

"To the Finland Station, I said!"

"I don't want Finland! Leningrad please!" I repeated like a parrot: "Leningrad please, Leningrad please!" I was almost crying.

But the ticket clerk said:

"Move away from the window. Don't block the line!"

I was almost hysterical, I moved away, still thinking to myself, wondering: Why does she keep saying Finland?

I couldn't understand, I had no idea at all what she was talking about.

My turn came round a second time. The ticket clerk said: "You again?"

I nodded and didn't say anything.

Anyway, she gave me a ticket. When I got the ticket, I went to the platform, then I looked at the ticket to see what was written on it. When I read it, my hair stood up on end. What it said on the ticket was Moscow–Helsinki. My God! Leningrad wasn't on it! I thought the ticket clerk must be either deaf or blind. I began to cry, but I kept on walking. I remember I showed the ticket to someone on the platform and they told me which train was mine and which track it was on. And now it was already time for it to leave. I ran up to the car and gave the ticket to the conductor at the door, went into the car, and straight into my compartment.

The conductor said:

"I'll wake you when we get to Leningrad."

I was exhausted after the long journey and the huge noisy waiting room in Moscow and the endless line. I was dog-tired, and so I fell asleep straightaway.

Early in the morning the conductor woke me up. I got out of the train. That day was June 13, 1983. There I was in

Leningrad, where the great tsars Peter the Great and Catherine the Great once ruled. There it was in front of my eyes, legendary, mighty Leningrad. And as for the ticket clerk, she was right, there was a Finland Station in Leningrad. And all because of Finland I'd spent two hours standing in line like a fool at the Leningrad Station in Moscow.

I walked along the street, and I saw a little railroad car coming toward me. I thought, are there really trains as small as that? I have to get into it. But it turned out to be a streetcar. I'd never been in any big cities before, not Tashkent or any other city.

The streetcar moved along. After three stops a young woman as thin as a skeleton came up to me and said:

"Your ticket?"

I didn't say anything.

She said:

"You have to pay a three-rouble fine."

I began to cry. There weren't many passengers in the streetcar. One man said:

"Inspector, why are you bothering her, can't you see she's crying?"

Another passenger, a woman, said:

"Look at her, all those braids! There must be forty of them."

The inspector said:

"Is this the first time you've been here, then?"

I nodded.

She said:

"What do you have in your town?"

I cried and said:

"We have donkeys and diesels." That was what we called buses.

The passengers in the streetcar listened to my explanation and laughed. The inspector said:

"Who have you come to see? Going to study, are you?"

"Hmm."

"In what college?"

"The university."

"Ha-ha, with Russian like that she wants to go to the university!"

I didn't say anything.

She told me again:

"Now you'll have to pay three roubles. And drop three kopecks in the box over there. You should have explained to me that this was your first time in the city. Look, I've already torn off your ticket for the fine."

I paid. I wonder how I was supposed to know I had to drop three kopecks in the box to pay for a ticket. In our kishlak we handed the money to the bus driver.

The young woman inspector looked at me with pity and said:

"And where are you going to go now?"

"The university."

"And do you know how to get there?"

"No."

"Then let me show you the way."

We got out of the car together and walked to a bus stop. At the bus stop she explained to me how to get to the university. We said good-bye and she put me on the bus.

I reached the university and found the building where my friends, the orientalist students, had their classes, the group that had been in Khiva. I went to the dean's office and said I was looking for some students—so-and-so and so-and-so. They told me that the students I was looking for had all gone away to the East on a field trip. After that answer, to be honest, I didn't know what to do. I went out into the street with my suitcase and asked myself: Where do I go now?

I walked up and down the sidewalks, like Lenin when he returned from exile. What next? I wondered. I walked for a while, got hungry, and went into a food store. They had everything you could think of in there! I went up to a sales assistant and pointed to a spice-cake, because I didn't know the word "spice-cake."

She said:

"What do you want?"

I didn't say anything, just pointed with my finger.

She said:

"You don't even know what you want to buy! Get out of here, don't hold up the line, time, time, people are waiting."

The shop had a check system—pay first, then take the check to the counter. Customers with checks were walking this way and that way to the different sections. But I had no idea what the system was like: why were they all walking about with little pieces of paper and standing in lines?

I spent quite a long time in the shop without getting anywhere, and I was hungry! Alas, it was in vain. I left that shop still feeling hungry. I hadn't had a hot meal for days.

I walked along the sidewalks and suddenly saw a woman in a white coat who was shouting:

"Hot piroshki with potato, with cabbage! Hot piroshki!"

She was selling piroshki right there in the street. I walked up to her and gave her money without saying anything. And she gave me a hot pastry without saying anything.

After the pastry I felt very thirsty. Where was the water? There wasn't any anywhere, even though all of Leningrad was built on water. But I had to be patient. I walked on. I saw people going into a tunnel where there was a big letter M. Is that a toilet, then? I thought. But why is there only M written on it—is it only for men? But there were women going in as well. I had no idea what it was.

Like curious Varvara in the folk proverbs, who lost her nose at the market, I went down the steps too. Well would you ever—it was the metro! Of course I started changing money, like everyone else. You dropped twenty kopecks or ten kopecks into the box and out came your change in five-kopeck coins.

I played for a long time, it was very interesting for a primitive savage like me!

Then I went to the entrance and tried to go down, but that machine (I found out later that it's called a turnstile) squeezed me so hard I screamed as if I was being killed. But it was my own fault, because I dropped five kopecks into the machine of one gate and tried to go through a different one. So of course it squeezed me! Luckily the inspector or controller, or whoever it was, came over and let me through the gate that wasn't working beside her little booth.

After that accident I was afraid to ride in the metro for a long time. That's the story of what happened.

I walked down the stairs to the cars. It was all the same to me which way I went. So I got into a car and set off. I don't know how many hours I was in the metro. I got out at one station, changed to the other platform and got in again, and rode like that—backward and forward. I didn't know how to get out of the metro.

I finally decided:

What difference does it make where I get out, I've nowhere to go anyway. Wherever I might be, I'm getting out. I walked out of the metro and found I was in the Lenin district, at the Baltic metro station.

All the time I wanted water, plain, simple water. Why plain water? Because I'd never drunk lemonade or Coca-Cola or champagne or wine or cognac or vodka. I've never tried them in my life, and I don't intend to. To this day I don't drink anything apart from plain water and green tea. No matter what's happening: a birthday, New Year's, a wedding, a party —I never drink.

I had no food in my suitcase, apart from the stale bread. I walked to the Warsaw Station, sat down in the waiting hall, and gnawed on my bread. I wondered what I ought to do. Those students I knew weren't there, and I didn't want to go back home, I'd be ashamed. I could imagine the welcome they'd give me. And my memories of my childhood weren't all that good . . .

I thought: No, there's no way back!

Suddenly I remembered something. They'd given me their addresses. I opened the suitcase and took out my address book. And one address was in Leningrad. It was the address of the Georgian, Giya, he lived on Warsaw Street.

I had to find that street, if I didn't want to be left out on the street myself. I asked people here, there, and everywhere, and I found the street. I went up to the second floor or the third, I don't remember now, and I stood in front of the door of the apartment. I knocked, although there was a special bell, but I wasn't used to ringing. A woman's voice answered from behind the door:

"Who's there?"

I knocked again. The same voice asked:

"Who's there?" And finally the door opened a little and a woman was standing there. "Who do you want?"

"Giya."

"What do you mean, Giya?"

"I want Giya!"

"What's that you say you want? Giya's not here, he's gone to the Far East."

I was nervous and I shouted:

"I saw, I saw, I saw!"

"What did you see? Who did you see? Ooph, I don't understand a thing! Who did you see?"

"I saw Giya."

"Girl, I told you, he's not here and he won't be for a long time!"

"I want Giya, I saw Giya!"

"Girl, go away, he's not here!"

I was almost crying, I could hardly stop myself. She sensed that and said:

"Who are you? Where from? Who have you come to see?"

"I Uzbekistan. I Bibish. I saw Giya. I want Giya."

"Maybe you've come to study?"

"Hmm." I nodded.

"Where are you going to study?"

"University."

"Which faculty?"

"History." I don't know where I got that idea from, but that was what I said.

"Girl, there's nothing I can do to help you. Giya's not here, and I can't let you in. Oh, take our telephone number, when you get settled, call us, all right? Maybe when Giya gets back you'll come to see us."

She went to write down the telephone number and came back out a few moments later.

"There's the number for you . . . Call, all right! Now excuse me, good-bye." Then she closed the door and locked it. And I was left in the lobby. When she slammed the door, it felt like someone had hit me. I went out into the street and started sobbing, I told myself: You fool, you fool, why did you come here?

I barely managed to calm myself. It was already late. About eleven o'clock in the evening, I suppose. I don't remember exactly. I rode on a streetcar for a long, long time. I got out of the streetcar, and there was the student hostel of the engineering institute on the bank of the bypass canal. I saw a fountain in the yard of the hostel. I dashed over to it and began drinking the dirty water. I had no option: my mouth was all dry.

Then I sat down on a bench and gnawed on my stale bread.

Suddenly I saw two elderly women walking toward the bench. They sat down beside me. After a few minutes they turned to me and asked:

"Do you study here, my girl?"

"No."

"Then why are you sitting out here so late? It's dark already, it's dangerous out on the street."

I didn't say anything.

"Oh, you've got such long braids! Where are you from?"

"Uzbekistan."

"Has something happened to you?"

I didn't say anything.

"And where are you going to spend the night?"

I didn't know the phrase "spend the night," so I shook my head to show I didn't understand the question.

"Where are you going to sleep?"

"Here."

"Don't be silly," said one of the women. "How can you do that, come with me to my place, my daughter. You can explain everything to me, tell me all about it, all right? Let's go, it's really very late."

"No." I refused. I thought they would trick me, and I was afraid they would take my money away from me. That was all I was concerned about.

The other woman said:

"It's dangerous to stay here, come with us, or you could get kidnapped, or raped, or killed, you know."

When I heard her say that, I agreed straightaway. I picked up the suitcase and went with them. One of them was called Svoboda Vasilievna, and the other was Aunty Tanya. Svoboda Vasilievna took me to her place. And Aunty Tanya sat with us for a while and went home. How good it is, I thought, that someone has given me shelter for tonight.

I was so tired, I slept like a log. I was absolutely exhausted. Early in the morning Svoboda Vasilievna gave me a sandwich to eat and black tea to drink. She spoke to me very kindly:

"You sit there like a deaf-mute. How are we going to find a common language, my daughter? I really don't know what to do."

Svoboda Vasilievna was a well-educated woman. She told me she had graduated from the Institute of Culture and worked in houses of culture, and now she was retired, but she still worked as the director of a children's club. And her friend Aunty Tanya worked in a movie theater, checking the tickets. Afterward, I remember, I went to the movies for free for a whole year.

Both women were energetic and determined. They discussed what to do with me and how to help me. Svoboda Vasilievna said:

"You need to get a job. You can always go back to your studies later, and anyway you don't know the language. I talk to you and you just gape at me, that's no way to carry on."

One day she came back from work with news:

"Bibish, I've been looking for a suitable job for you. They don't take on yardkeepers with diplomas." (I had a diploma, and I had to work off the cost of that diploma. If I took a job as a yardkeeper, they'd have had to give me a room in a communal apartment straightaway.) "I can get you a job as a nanny in a kindergarten. Pack your things, and we'll go out to a dacha in Komarovo. A friend of mine is the director. And the children are there for three months, for the summer. I'll ask the director to take you on. Do you understand at least?"

I nodded like I always did.

The next day I went to the dacha in Komarovo with Svoboda Vasilievna. She talked to the director about me. Anyway, the director agreed to give me a job as a nanny. Svoboda Vasilievna encouraged me and went back to the city. And I stayed at the dacha.

The director was a harsh and strict woman. Even when there was no need, she always shouted at everybody, and so the people who worked there were always leaving. The kindergarten was always short of either a teacher or a nanny. That was why she gave me a job straightaway, even without a residence permit. After all, when I made up my mind to run away to Leningrad I was in such a great hurry that I didn't even cancel my registration at home.

The director showed me the junior group I would be working with as a nanny.

And I started working in the kindergarten. Of course, the director explained what my duties were. On the whole, it wasn't difficult working as a nanny. I got the work done, and everything was fine. I got to know the girls working there: Anna Petrovna—I am still in touch with her, after twenty years. Olya, Lena, Tamara, Galya . . .

When the cooks at the kindergarten found out I didn't know Russian very well, they decided to have a joke with me.

One day they called me:

"Bibish, come here! Do you know what monthlies are?"

"No, I don't."

"Then take this bucket, go to the director, and ask her to give you a bucketful of monthlies, all right?"

"All right, I'll go straightaway."

I took the bucket and went to the director's office. I knocked at the door. She said:

"Come in!"

I went in, held the bucket out toward her, and said calmly:

"Zinaida Alexandrovna, please give me one monthlies bucket."

"What's that?" She even got halfway out of her chair.

"Give me one monthlies bucket."

"What monthlies! What are you saying? That's disgusting, who sent you?"

"The cooks."

"Right, then, send them to me, and I'll show them! My monthlies finished a long time ago, let them bring a bucket of their own!"

What a commotion there was!

After that some time went by and the cooks started again:

"Bibish, go and tell the director she's a pompous gasbag! Go on!"

And again, like a fool, I went—can you imagine!

I knocked at the door of the office, but this time the cooks came running up and just managed to stop me in time:

"Don't say anything, we were only having a joke."

One day the teacher of my group came up to me and said:

"Bibish, Maxim's pooped in his pants, take them off and clean it all up!"

"What?"

"Maxim's pooped in his pants!"

It was the first time I'd heard the word "pooped," and I said to her:

"I don't understand, what does 'pooped' mean?"

The poor thing—she said:

"What? How can you not understand, it's elementary, people poop. Maxim for instance, or you, or anyone else."

"I don't know. What's 'pooped'?"

She began getting nervous:

"My God, you must understand that: when someone eats, afterward they have to poop, now do you understand?"

"No."

She was getting really hysterical now and tried to explain a different way.

"When a person does poo-poo!"

It was only then that I realized what "pooped" meant.

* * *

Anyway, I worked and relaxed at the dacha for three months, and then we came back to the city, and I continued working for the same kindergarten in the city. I lived with Svoboda Vasilievna, but I was still like a deaf-mute. She gave me a few lessons in Russian. She gave me assignments: I wrote dictations, and she corrected the mistakes. Sometimes she encouraged me, sometimes she scolded me. That was how I gradually learned Russian. There in the city the cooks began making fun of me again.

One day, I remember, two cooks came running up to me and said:

"Bibish, do you know what a lecturer is?"

"No, I don't. What's a lecturer?"

"You know, Bibish, a lecturer is a kind of profession, how can I explain . . . In a word, a lecturer is someone who checks who's a virgin and who isn't. He checked us a long time ago already, and now it's your turn. He'll come in a minute to check you, understand? There's the table, take your panties off, lie down, open your legs wide, and wait for the lecturer, understand?"

"Yes, I understand."

They ran away, and even though I felt uneasy, I did what they'd said: I took my panties off, lay down on the table, and opened my legs wide. I lay there on the table with no panties on waiting for that lecturer. And I was dreadfully afraid that I wasn't a virgin and now everyone would know about it. My heart started beating so hard I thought it would leap out of my chest.

I lay there and several minutes went past. There was nothing, silence. So I just went on lying there.

Then suddenly the door opened, and there was a man wearing a tie, with some kind of file under his arm. I lifted my head up a bit and looked at him from where I was lying. My heart started beating even faster. He just stood there, and his eyes opened as wide as headlamps. The poor man stood there and didn't move, not a muscle. He looked at me, and he seemed to be surprised, and I looked at him, and I was surprised too, and I wondered why he didn't come over to me and check if I was a virgin or not. It was strange!

But he stood there just like a statue.

Eventually the director came up behind him and screamed:

"This is outrageous! All right, get up!"

Of course, I was startled and confused. I got up quickly, put on my panties, and looked at the man. The poor creature was still standing there with his mouth open. And the director said:

"Go on, call all the teachers and nannies, quickly, I want them all to come here!" Of course, I called everyone to join the group. They all came and sat on the chairs. And the man in the tie went up to the table where I was lying earlier, opened his file, took some papers out of it, and started talking about something, I don't remember what it was now. And he kept looking at me.

I thought: Why didn't he come over to me? It's strange, why is he reading some papers or other? Why didn't he check me?

Afterward they told me a lecturer reads lectures and doesn't check girls. And like a fool I'd been lying there on the table without any panties on and with my legs open wide.

In the kindergarten I worked until three o'clock in the afternoon. And I was still living with Svoboda Vasilievna. She had a friend, or partner—Uncle Zhora, a ballet-master. His apartment was in a different district, but he often visited Svoboda Vasilievna and stayed for the night, or even lived there for weeks at a time. Sometimes, even quite often, he would arrive drunk and start yelling and kick me out into the street.

And then the fall came. It was already November. One day Uncle Zhora arrived drunk and put on his usual performance and started a fight with Svoboda Vasilievna. They quarreled very badly. And then he attacked me and again kicked me out. I took offense and ran outside in nothing but my thin housecoat and my slippers. I walked along, crying. It was a Saturday. The kindergarten was closed for two days.

I walked round the railroad stations, wandered round the streets, and I didn't have a kopeck in my pocket. It was already evening and very dark. Then I sat in the waiting hall at a railroad station, but not for long, because the militiamen were checking people's documents and tickets. I wandered around in the cold until the morning, but I didn't go back to Svoboda Vasilievna's apartment. Then I suddenly remembered Anna Petrovna's address—she was a teacher at the kindergarten.

Early on Sunday morning, on the second day, I went to her. She was very upset and said:

"I'd be glad to let you stay with me, but besides me, my sister and her fiancé also live here, and it's very crowded." It was true—she lived in a communal apartment.

And I had to go back out on the street again.

It was very cold in my thin housecoat and slippers. It was the second night I hadn't slept. Before morning came I must have walked round all of Leningrad. I was hungry and cold. Early on Monday morning I came to the kindergarten and ran round and round it so I wouldn't freeze. At about six o'clock the cooks came and opened the door. I dashed toward them straightaway. They saw me and asked:

"Bibish, why are you here so early, why have you turned blue, why are you so lightly dressed?"

But I didn't have the strength to answer them. They opened the door, I went in and fell over in the lobby. When I came round I saw I was in the closet, that is, in the little room where the mattresses were kept. They must have dragged me in there so I could catch up on my sleep. I slept for a whole day and night. No one woke me up. When I came round, the teachers advised me:

"Go to the director. Say she must give you a place to live. You can't go on like this, you'll kill yourself."

I went to the director:

"Zinaida Alexandrovna, I'd like to ask you if I can have a room in a communal apartment to go with my job, please help me."

But she shouted angrily:

"I know you people! First you work and then, as soon as you get a place to live, you hand in your notice straightaway, and who's going to work for me? No one! You can't have a room. I heard you spent two days wandering round the streets, but what can I do about it?" She paused and then said: "All right, I'm not made of iron, I'll allow you to live here, in the kindergarten, stay after work and live here. In the evenings the watchman, Borya, comes, and the two of you can guard the kindergarten. Now go and work."

I was really delighted that now I wouldn't have to hang about outside at night and wander the streets until morning came.

From that day on I stayed in the kindergarten after work. I lived on the second floor in my group's classroom. The watchman Uncle Borya said:

"It's a good thing the director said you can stay here. I'll be able to go home now. Only don't you tell the director."

And so he always went away, and I was left alone. And he also warned me:

"Don't keep the light on, or the drunks might throw a bottle through the window."

And so I used to stay in there without any light until the morning. I always ate cold food, what was left over from the children's meals, or from the ones who hadn't come to the kindergarten. On Saturday and Sunday I was almost always hungry, because what I saved wasn't enough for two days.

At that kindergarten I was reminded of my own preschool in the kishlak. A government commission checked it every so often. When the teachers heard the commission was coming to check them, they went out "hunting" with their director. They looked for children everywhere. When they found some, they tried to persuade our parents to let us attend the kindergarten temporarily. As soon as the commission left, we were sent home straightaway. At least we got a chance to eat something nice while the check was going on, but afterward they stopped feeding us properly. Sometimes I had to go to the kindergarten even when there wasn't a commission. Then what the caretakers did was first eat the main dish in the office with their own children and give us just the soup with nothing else, and so we didn't want to go to the kindergarten. We tried to go only when they had a commission, so we could have something nice to eat. But they begged only the parents to bring their children so that the kindergarten wouldn't be closed. And they always got away with it.

* * *

And so I lived like that for eight months, all alone in the kindergarten in the evenings, without anyone else.

Sometimes I went into the city for a little while, to the long-distance public telephones, to call home. To reassure them, I said I'd got into the university and was already attending classes.

It was difficult. The low pay was never enough. The money ran out very quickly. In the streetcar I always tried to stand next to the ticket dispenser, and when people handed on the money for a ticket to me, I tore one off for myself as well, making sure no one saw me. It was shameful, but what else could I do?

And I remember, when I was living in the kindergarten, one of the teachers used to come every Saturday and Sunday and call up to my window: "Are you still alive?" She used to bring me hot tea in a thermos. I was so glad when she came! At least there was someone to say a few words to.

Winter came. It was cold. All the ground was covered with snow. The black ice made it impossible to walk. Once I went into the city to buy an envelope. I walked along the narrow paths that had been swept clean in order not to fall.

Suddenly I heard a voice, an old granny calling:

"Daughter, help me, give me your hand!"

I didn't know that in Russian the word for meant "pen" could mean "hand" too. I answered:

"I haven't got a pen," and continued walking, thinking how I should have brought a pencil with me. Then I looked round and saw the old granny was sitting on the snow, trying to get up.

I went back to her and helped her up, and she said:

"Good, thank you, at last you understood!"

I often used my "knowledge" of Russian in the wrong way. This is what happened another time:

I already knew that Leningraders are cultured people, and they talk to each other very politely. And I wanted be like them. One day I got into a bus to go somewhere. There were a lot of people in the bus. And then one of the passengers, a woman, sneezed. I turned round and said:

"Bless you!"

And she replied rudely:

"Mind your own business!"

After that answer I never tried to be polite in public transport again.

So that was how I lived in the city of Leningrad.

One day I decided to phone Giya, the student who lived on Warsaw Street, the one I went looking for during my first days in Leningrad, and his mother wouldn't let me into the apartment. His mother answered:

"Yes, yes, hello."

"Is Giya there?"

"Who's asking for him?"

"I'm Bibish."

"What Bibish?"

"The one from the East, from Khiva."

"Wait, wait, the one with the braids? Right?"

"Yes, that's me."

"Where are you, for God's sake, don't hang up!"

"All right. I'm calling from work, from a kindergarten."

"Why didn't you call sooner, how could you do that? I gave you the number!"

"I didn't want to bother you, especially with Giya not there."

"Bibish, when he came back from the East, of course I told him you'd arrived, and he asked: 'Where is she then?' I said: 'I don't know, she was going to join the history faculty, or maybe some other.' And he got angry and said: 'Oh, mom, what have you gone and done! Bibish's mother had nine children, but she spent days and days helping us in Khiva! And she spent her own money, she took us to a party, she saw us off to the railroad station, she gave us souvenirs. You can barely manage just to bring me up, and now with all your principles, you've sent her back out onto the street! Mom, how could you? She doesn't know the city, if she came here, it's because I gave her the address. Mom, think what you've done! Now where can I look for her?' Then I went to the university and looked for you everywhere in the lists of applicants who got in or didn't get in, but it was all futile. He reproached me every day because of you. But I was still hoping you would phone. Can you hear me, Bibish, can you come to visit us? What a nice surprise it would be for Giya!"

"I can hear you, thank you, I'll definitely come, only I can't come today."

"Then when will you come?"

"Let's say the day after tomorrow, five o'clock."

"All right, we'll be expecting you. Only before you come, call first, all right?"

"All right, I'll definitely come."

That was how our long conversation finished. Two days later I called and Giya answered. He was delighted and said he would meet me outside in the street. So I went visiting.

He really was waiting for me with flowers, and when we met he kissed me. His mother, father, and grandmother were waiting for me at home. They fed me Georgian food. The conversation wasn't working out though, because of me. Giya's mother kept saying how Giya had tormented her and how she'd looked everywhere for me. And I sat there without saying anything, listening, and just nodding my head.

Then Giya said:

"This won't get us anywhere, just a minute, I'll be back."

He went out. After half an hour he came back with a girl with a dark complexion and said:

"There, I've brought you an interpreter. Now I hope you'll understand each other. This is Rano, a Leningrad University student from Tajikistan."

This girl had very long, beautiful braids. Well, of course, with an interpreter it was easier for all of us. Poor Rano translated. She did the best she could, because she was Tajiki, and I'm Uzbeki, and the languages are different. The Tajik language belongs to the Persian group, and the Uzbek language belongs to the Turkish group. Luckily Rano could speak a little Uzbek. A few years later she and Giya got married.

After supper they wouldn't let me go, and I stayed in their home for the night. In the morning Giya's mother invited me to go for a walk round the city.

"I'm so ashamed, you were probably left out on the street because of me, Bibish," she said and started to cry.

I think she worked as a research assistant in some institute, I don't remember now.

I told her about myself, and then she said:

"But if you're living in that kindergarten without any light or any food, that's very bad. I'll ask Giya, maybe he'll find a place for you in the hostel with the students in his year."

We walked round the city, then went home and waited for Giya. He came back after his classes, his mother explained everything to him, and Giya and I went to the hostel. I saw my old friends Zarina and Svetlana there. We remembered how we met and had a good laugh. The girls agreed to do what Giya asked and let me stay in their room in the hostel. They arranged things with the doorkeeper, and she always let me through. So it was all right.

* * *

I worked in the kindergarten until three o'clock, and straightaway after work I ran to the hostel. I got to know more students: Berid from Germany, Tkho and Lok from Vietnam, Arkasha and Bator from Mongolia, Ira from Buryatia. I remember I used to bring the girls food that was left over at the kindergarten after the children's meals: rissoles, apples, omelettes . . . You know, students are always hungry.

And everything was fine, until they changed the doorkeeper in the hostel. Now the new doorkeeper asked everyone for their passes. One fine day she refused to let me in and said: "Show me your student card." But I didn't have one, so I was left out on the street again.

To be honest, I didn't want to bother anyone anymore, so I simply walked away from the hostel and wandered the streets again until the morning, like a tramp. I was frozen and exhausted and I thought: Why does everything turn out like this for me? Why is my life so cursed, and what's the point in living if it's like this?

And so I walked on and on round the streets, then I stopped and lay down on the concrete so that a car would run over me. I lay there and waited. I couldn't care less about anything, I just wanted to die as soon as possible, that was all.

Suddenly a car stopped. A man jumped out of it, ran up to me, and shouted:

"You shouldn't drink so much! These young people nowadays!"

I lay there and cried and I didn't answer.

He half lifted me up from the road.

"But you're sober!"

I didn't say anything.

"All right, get up!"

"I won't, I want to die."

"Enough of that! You've plenty of time to die. It's all ahead of you, get up. Where shall I take you?" He helped me to stand up.

"To the bypass canal embankment, that's where I want to go."

"Another fine idea! Now you're going to drown yourself?"

"No, I already tried to drown myself. It didn't work. Someone I know lives near the bypass canal."

"That's a different matter. Let's go then."

And so there I was, still alive.

I went to see Anna Petrovna. She introduced me to a friend of hers, and I lived with her for a while.

But how long could I keep on wandering from one stranger to another? One day I came to work and told Anna Petrovna I was really desperate and asked what I should do.

She sighed and said:

"Listen, go and see the Duma deputy for our district. Kirill Lavrov, the People's Artist of the USSR. Perhaps he'll help you."

So I went for a consultation with the deputy Kirill Lavrov, but when I saw him in the corridor, so handsome in his suit and tie, I felt embarrassed and went back to the kindergarten.

I suffered like that for about ten months. Then I had to leave my job and go back to my native parts, to my kishlak in Uzbekistan. What else could I do now, with no apartment or work or place to study? Nothing had worked out for me. I had no money, I didn't know Russian, and I had no one to support me. I didn't want to be a burden to my friends, they all had their own lives. It made me feel so sick to go back! But what else was there left for me to do? I had to accept it. And that was all.

I remember I didn't even have any money to get back. Giya and the other students and Genriko Sergeevna collected the money for the ticket. I said good-bye to them and got into the train. I traveled for three and a half days without eating, because I had no money left.

I barely made it home.

The kishlak again, and all the same people, the same glances, the same gossip. Hard times were beginning at home just then. There was no money, barely enough even for bread.

One day I found out that one of our neighbors had gone to the city of Samarqand and danced there at weddings and brought back a lot of money. Straightaway I thought: Why shouldn't I go and earn money at weddings? In the East they give huge money to dancers. Since I couldn't dance where they knew me, I went away to a different region. After all, if anyone found out that I danced at weddings, no one would marry me.

I was eighteen. Stupid and naive. It's very hard for a young girl without experience to go and dance at a wedding. I found out in secret the best way to get to Samarqand, how to find the right address, and where to stay. Then I went to earn some money.

I found the right address, and the right house. The mistress of the house didn't waste any time being polite—she looked me over from head to toe and said I would do. She asked me to show her my dancing costume. I told her:

"I don't have a dancing costume."

She reassured me:

"Don't worry about that, I have some suitable material, you can have it and take it to a dressmaker."

"But I don't have any money."

"That doesn't matter. You'll earn some, and then we'll settle up."

Apart from me, another four girls were living in the room the mistress put me in, young girls, and they were from different regions too.

The next day I went to the dressmaker, and soon my dress for performing was ready. It was a very beautiful dress.

And then the mistress sent me to a wedding with an accompanist for the first time. I should tell you about these musicians who play at weddings. They keep a close eye on the dancers to make sure they don't hide the money they get, but give it all to the mistress. If they notice that a girl hides part of the money, she's fired straightaway. And they used to give me so much money, more than I could hold in my hands! I'd never seen so much money in my life. A genuine dancer at weddings has to know how to dance beautifully and flirtatiously, so they'll give her a lot of money. For the other men not to pester the dancer, the musician will often say that she's his girlfriend. Sometimes they really did have several wives.

So anyway, my mistress took more money than usual from the musician because I was new. And she said to me:

"Keep a journal, write down how much you've earned each evening. And I'll keep a journal too. When you want to leave, I'll give you all your money."

How wonderful, I thought, I'll have my own money, and I'll be able to help my father!

And so there I was at the wedding. Before we went out into the courtyard where the people were sitting, we were fed very tasty food. There was mutton and all sorts of different fruits: pomegranates, apples, pears, apricots, peaches, watermelons, melons—anything we liked, we could eat everything.

When I went out to dance the first time, I was trembling all over, I was feeling afraid, I suppose. But then, when they started giving me money one after another, I began feeling stronger. And I told myself: Hold on, you came here to earn money, there it is, the money you've dreamed about all your life!

I put this huge amount of money in the instrument case and went back to dance. It went on like that until midnight. Then they fed the dancers again and called us into a room where some kind of bigshots were sitting. And I danced for the bigwigs, and they gave me lots of money too. It was more money than I'd ever dreamed of. Although, at first, until I got used to it, all the dancing made me terribly tired.

That first day I wrote down how much money I earned in my journal straightaway. And so things went on. When according to my count I'd already earned a lot of money, I wanted to go home as soon as possible, but the season wasn't over.

There's something else that I ought to say. Nowadays in Russia and in the West belly dancing is fashionable. Specially trained young girls dance in a sexy way to the music of Arabian and Turkish dances, without even knowing what they're about. They're used to it, they earn good money. It's just a show to them. Well, of course, people have to live. But it upsets me that they bring shame on the entire East with this. After all, apart from this sexy belly dance, our eastern dances use movements of the arms and the head and facial expressions to tell the story of our lives and our culture: about picking cotton, weaving carpets, about our gardens and our vines . . . These dances express the states of the soul—both joy and sadness. But on television they mostly show girls with bare stomachs jerking their navels about, and that's all.

After about a month and a half, I decided I had enough money. According to my notes I could buy a new Zhiguli, that is, an entire car. But the mistress had all the money. And my passport as well. So when I decided to go home I went to the mistress and said to her:

"Aunty, please give me my money, I'm going to go home."

She answered:

"Don't be in a hurry. Work a bit more. Why are you in such a rush to go back into poverty?"

"No, I've done enough. I'm tired already, now let the other girls earn money."

"But they're leaving too. All right, wait, I'll just be a moment."

She went into her room and came back a few minutes later:

"There's your money and your passport."

I took the passport and started counting the money in front of her. My God, I was horrified! There were only thirteen hundred roubles, where was the rest? You see, I'd earned about six thousand Lenin roubles. Everything I'd earned was written down in my journal. Why was there so little? And I said:

"Aunty, where's the rest of the money?"

She answered in a very harsh, brazen voice:

"What money? That's it, there isn't any more money. In the first place, you came here illegally! In the second place, I arranged everything, if it wasn't for me, you'd have died of hunger! I pay off the militia too. Do you think it's easy for me to keep you all here? Take what you're given and get lost!"

By the end I was shouting. But what could I say to her?

I had to take the money she gave me. Even that much was my father's salary for a year. But if I'd got all of my six thousand roubles, it would have been my father's salary for five years.

You can't imagine what a state I was in: What about all my hard work! I'd really sweated for that money. And in the end all I got was a miserly thirteen hundred roubles.

I had to leave quickly, so the mistress wouldn't think up some kind of nasty trick. It turned out that I wasn't the only one the mistress had swindled, she'd done it to everyone who was living with her. She'd stolen from them all in the same way and put it in her own pocket.

After this happened I couldn't bear even to hear the word "dance," and I didn't dance again for a long time, because I kept remembering that woman. Even if I'd wanted to dance somewhere else in some other region, where could I go, who could I turn to? I couldn't go back to the same swindler again.

If it happened to me all over again now and I was still eighteen years old, I don't know what I would do.

But one thing I do know: people have to do what they can do well. And before that I was always ordered about by my brothers and other relatives, who forbade me to dance and sing and meet boys and go to the movies . . . I had no life of my own before. My brothers always told me what I should do and what I shouldn't. They were terribly afraid of gossip. But I was simply a little girl who wanted to dance. And no one understood me. Let me tell you, when you feel out of place, it's frustrating. But when they won't let you find your own place, it's far worse.

In our village they didn't even allow people to sing, let alone dance. Of course, I can't sing, I have no voice. But I can dance —to any music. When I was young I could have earned huge money with my talent, but my relatives were afraid of the disgrace. According to them, it was better to live in poverty than allow me to dance at weddings and parties. But even when I was asleep I used to invent different movements and expressions, I made up entire productions. Then in the morning, I got up—and what could I do? Who would have let me bring my ideas to life?

Perhaps I was born in the wrong place at the wrong time, I don't know. But that's what my life was like: not really my own.

THE LEGEND OF GRIEF

One day God decided to test the strength of grief. First he sent grief to the sea, he wanted to test the sea. The sea dried up. Then he inflicted grief on the mountains. The mountains collapsed and crumbled into little stones. He sent grief to the desert. A sandstorm blew up in the desert and scattered all the sand, and nothing was left of the desert. God didn't know what to do next. "All right now," he thought, "I'll test grief on man. Let's see what happens to him." And he sent grief to man. But man did not dry up, like the sea. He did not collapse, like the mountains. He did not disappear, like the desert. Man suffered terrible torment from grief, but he carried on living. Because he knew how to suffer, but he also knew how to rejoice. God realized that only man could bear grief, and he left it with people.

Without joy it is impossible to live. Without joy you grow old straightaway. The longer I live, the more I want to give joy to people, to distract them from the vain hustle and bustle of life so that they can forget their worries and relax for at least a little while. After all, some fine day we're all going to die. It's better to bring people joy than cause them terrible pain.

Those are the thoughts I live with now. But it's not always possible to bring people joy. Sometimes you want to do something nice for someone, and for some reason they reject you or belittle you. It happens. I used to get offended, but I'm more resilient now. I can put up with it—what can you do, that's the way life is.

Now the time has come to tell you about my marriage. You already know that in the East, if you're not a virgin anymore, they punish you for it. You are like spoiled goods. And they pay *kalym,* a bride price, for you, they hold a wedding, and so the bridegroom's family spends a lot of money. If they find out that you weren't a virgin when you got married, they can take back the kalym, and they'll sit you backward on a donkey and ride you around the entire district like that. I always suffered because I thought no one would marry me the way I was.

And so, after my adventures in Leningrad, I went back to Uzbekistan, to my native kishlak. I took a job where my father worked, in the school, as an elementary class teacher. For the summer vacation I decided to go to my mother's uncle. He lived with his family in Turkmenia, in the town of Tashauz (it's called Dashhowuz now), and I had a girlfriend who lived in that town.

And so I went to visit them. I was given a warm welcome at my uncle's house and at my girlfriend's, after all we didn't see each other very often: it was such a long way, and it was a different republic too.

* * *

One day my girlfriend and I were strolling round the town. We met three boys beside the movie theater. One of them took a fancy to my friend, and I took a fancy to him. That boy was my future husband. My friend always dressed well, in beautiful things. But what did I have, apart from my long braids? I was plain and ordinary, poorly dressed . . . In other words, homely, a freak.

The boys invited us to the movies, but we refused, it was time for us to go home. But we arranged to meet them three days later. On the way home my friend told me those boys lived nearby and she'd often seen them. It turned out the first one was called Marsel, the second was Ikram, but she didn't know the third one's name. They were from rich families. They were boys who didn't go short of anything. I said:

"It's all right for them, with rich parents, they eat what they like and wear what they like."

But my friend said:

"It just seems that way. Everyone has his own life. Little people have little problems, big people have big problems, so it's better not to envy anyone."

For three days the only thing I thought about was when we would meet them. I "rented out" a dress from my friend. But alas, the meeting never took place. My friend's mother was irritable, she wouldn't let us go. I was so upset, I thought that now I'd never see Ikram again.

But I was wrong. A week later I met him by chance, only it didn't come to anything. He'd obviously taken a fancy to my friend, and she wasn't with me. So we just said good-bye.

Afterward I found out from my friend exactly where he lived and every day I lay in wait for when he would come out. And when he came out of the house and went either straight on, or left, or right, I immediately walked round the houses, the road, and the sidewalk and ended up walking toward him as if nothing was going on and it was a chance meeting. But in fact I was already head over heels in love with him. And then one day he did ask me to go for a walk with him, and I was so glad I agreed straightaway. After the walk he saw me home to my friend's house.

We met each other like that for a whole week. One day Ikram invited me out into the country, we walked through a mulberry grove, sat on the grass, looked at the sky, and gazed at the stars. We hugged and kissed each other. Anyway, that evening everything happened . . .

Then Ikram asked:

"How come, when you're from a rural area, where their ways are so strict, you're not a virgin anymore?" And he kept asking how it had happened.

I didn't tell him how it had really happened, I simply answered:

"A bastard raped me and didn't marry me, he just abandoned me!"

I didn't want to tell him my real story, it was too horrible to remember it.

Ikram said:

"Never mind, you can go to Baku or Tashkent, they'll sew you up, and you'll be a virgin again, like before. Lots of girls do that now. Then you'll make a good marriage."

I nodded in reply, but my heart felt heavy. He carried on comforting me, then he asked:

"Do you want to go to university? My uncle's the dean of the history faculty in Tashkent University. Let me give you his address."

"No thanks, I'll do it myself."

It was very late already, and he walked me home to my friend's house. On the way neither of us said anything. In front of the house he stopped me and said his telephone number out loud so that I would remember it, and he repeated it a few times. That was how we parted.

What could I hope for? He was handsome and high-spirited with gray eyes and a white face, not like mine. He spoke Uzbek badly because he'd graduated from a Russian school and his mother was half Russian. I found out his father also spoke Russian, in other words they were a cultured family. And I could hardly speak a single word of Russian. There was a big distance between us.

But no one, no one, had ever kissed me so tenderly, and in general no one had ever treated me the way he did. I went to my friend and told her everything (not absolutely everything, of course). She listened to me closely and told me:

"He'll never marry you. He was probably just toying with you. He can see you're an ignorant country girl from a collective farm, so he wanted to try his luck. Don't you trust him, he has heaps more like you in the town."

After that I went home in despair. I was suffering so much for my love, and what was the point? I decided to leave my job in the school and go to a college. I took all my documents and went away to Tashkent. My father had begun building a new house, and he scolded me for not helping him. But he could tell that I was going to run away anyway and do what I wanted. I'm a Capricorn—as stubborn as a goat.

A day later I was in Tashkent. Straightaway I started looking for the pedagogical institute. I found it and looked at the announcements that listed the exams for each faculty. My God, you had to take math for almost every faculty, and math was always my weak subject!

I walked out of the pedagogical institute and found an apartment not far away. Then I went to the theatrical institute—it was hopeless, there were lots of applicants for every place, I had almost no chance at all, so what point was there in even risking it?

I set out to wander the city. I found the Institute of Culture and looked at the announcements there too—to see what the exams were. For the directing faculty you had to recite a monologue, for the methodology you had to write a script, and for the choreography faculty you had to dance.

I thought: That's good, I'll dance once and get in. And I handed in my documents to apply for the choreography faculty. When the consultations began before the exams I turned out to be one of the front-runners, an outstanding student: after all, I'd graduated from the pedagogical college, and all the others had graduated from only the ten-year school. And so I joined the Institute of Culture.

After the entrance exams, I went home until classes began in September. I thought it would make my parents happy that now I was a student in a higher educational institution. But they weren't happy at all, on the contrary, they abused me, because it was the choreography faculty and not the pedagogical institute. My brother wanted to beat me.

"I'll kill you, you're not going anywhere, it isn't enough for you to bring shame on us with your dancing, now you want to lead a dance group as well, is that it?" he shouted.

I had to calm them down and say that after a year I'd transfer to an external course in a different faculty, to study methodology and administration.

Only three days were left until the first of September, and I went back to Tashkent. Ahead of me there were classes, obstacles to overcome, tests, exams.

One day I decided to call Ikram, the boy I met in Turkmenia, but they didn't put me through, because no one answered. I'd been given a place in the student hostel: I was sharing a room with a Tajiki girl called Matlyuba. She was good and kind. Then I went with the students to the cotton fields. They took us to the Djizak steppes, where we picked the cotton. There were watermelon fields nearby, and the students ate watermelons all day long. It was great fun.

We came back to Tashkent three months later. Classes began. One day I went to the long-distance public telephone booth and called Ikram again. The exchange connected me and a woman answered. It was my future mother-in-law, Aunty Raya. I said:

"Hello, can I speak to Ikram?"

She called him.

"Hello," he said.

"Hello, do you remember me? It's Bibish, from Khiva."

"Of course I remember you, hello, how are things, where are you calling from?"

"I'm calling from Tashkent."

"Yes? How did you get there?"

"I joined an institute, I'm a student now."

"Congratulations. If you have time now, tell me your address, I'll write to you."

I gave him the information, and he promised to come. After that call I felt very happy somehow. I didn't know why. But afterward I thought: What will he come for, just for a visit, or with some serious intention that he didn't have before? I didn't know what that might mean. Perhaps he would come just to see his uncle?

I finished the first year. Studying was sometimes easy and sometimes difficult. We had classical dance and ballet as subjects. And I found time to write stories too.

The Story of My Stories

I began writing stories when I was still in school, probably in about the sixth grade. When I showed them to my father, he said:

"Very weak, write more."

But my mother said it would be better if I helped out around the house, and she beat me with the broom for my laziness. I liked to read books: Alexandre Dumas, Chingiz Aitmatov, Valentin Katayev, the *Mahabarata,* Aziz Nesin, Veniamin Kaverin, Maxim Gorky, all the volumes of *The Thousand and One Nights.* I read all these books in the Uzbek language.

My mother was angry, she said a book wasn't bread, it wouldn't feed you, and she forced me to do the housework. Because in our kishlaks mothers prepare the girls for marriage: they teach them to cook, to wash and clean. So that the future relatives won't say: "Her mother didn't teach her anything!"

In Central Asia the moon shines brightly at night. You can read by it. And so I made use of this moonlight and enjoyed reading various different books when everyone was sleeping. My mother scolded me again and said I could damage my eyes like that.

Once I took the stories that I had written in college to show to our teacher of Uzbek literature. He was surprised and said:

"You write stories, and I write poems! Leave me your story, and I'll read it at home."

Soon he brought back my story with corrections, invited me to the literature department, and said:

"I phoned a friend of mine, he's a writer, and he's published several books. I told him about you. Go to see him tomorrow with your story in the Union of Writers at five o'clock. And today I invite you to go for a walk with me."

I was upset by this announcement. I didn't know how to answer, because I hadn't expected anything like that from him. He sensed that and he said:

"We'll go to a certain place not far from here. All right?"

I was tormented by doubt: where was he planning to take me? Perhaps he invited all the girl students on walks? I didn't know what to do. But then I thought: All right, here goes—and I agreed.

He met me after classes and we set off. He told me where he was from and how he had gone to study in the teachers training college, he told me that he wrote poems and presented a program about literature on the television. He said he had six children, and his wife didn't work.

We walked on like that, and I was wondering where he was taking me. But he kept telling me about his poems and about different writers.

And then we came to something like a park. A place surrounded by a wall. Inside there was a long road, and at the end of it I could see some kind of building. When we came close, I saw a terrace with lots and lots of beds on it. And I saw toys dangling from the ceiling on strings.

I didn't understand anything at all. There were children of different ages. Some of them were lying on the beds, and some were sitting up.

My teacher said:

"Hadjar, why have you stopped? Let's go closer to the children, don't be afraid, they're not infectious."

And he said hello to the children and the women in white coats. Then he sat on one boy's bed and asked:

"How are you, little one, getting better? Do your mom and dad come to see you?"

I looked around. Some of the children were playing with the dangling toys. Some were lying there indifferently. They didn't feel like laughing.

We stayed there for a while and then walked to the door. On the way back he said to me:

"Some of these children are paralyzed, some have various

diseases of the bones. Some of them are beyond any help by medicine. They'll never be able to walk. Now you have seen them, Hadjar. So thank God that you walk across the ground on your own feet and always feel them supporting you. What is our grief in comparison with theirs?"

I felt so ashamed of my bad thoughts about my teacher!

The next day at five o'clock I was already at the Union of Writers. I found the office where the man my teacher had told me about was sitting. He asked me:

"Have you been writing for long?"

"Since sixth grade."

"What exactly?"

"Stories."

"What about?"

"About life. About childhood."

"All right, show me."

I took two ordinary exercise books out of my bag and showed them to him. He leafed through one and read a bit, a very little bit, then said:

"Well, what can I tell you? I agreed to see you, because someone I respect a lot asked me to. But your stories don't follow any rules. So don't be offended, but there's nothing I can do to help you."

I came back from seeing him as desolated and shattered as if someone in my family had died. When my teacher heard that they hadn't taken my stories, he said:

"Don't stop, write anyway. I'll have a word with the head of a literary studio so that you can go to the classes there."

"But I was told quite clearly that I don't know any of the rules about how to write!"

"Well, you'll learn that from him."

But I didn't go to those classes. Although I did go back to writing, but only much later.

One day I got a letter from Ikram. He asked if I had got married and asked me to write to him about it. I was very surprised: did he want to get married then? Oh, if he did, that was good! I answered that I was studying and I hadn't got married yet. That soon I was going to transfer to the extramural department and study to be a teaching methods specialist. And I also wrote that I was going to go home to Khiva and get a job, and I told him when the exam session for extramural students would start and gave him my home address so that he could write me a letter there later.

I went back home to my kishlak and got a job as the leader of the club in the collective farm. I organized dance circles and knitting circles. The pay was pitiful. Several times I tried to organize a show, but apart from a few school students, no one came to the club, and their parents forbade them to come to the dance circle. And so for days on end I had nothing to do at work: I mostly felt tired because of the heat, I used to lock the door of my office from the inside and sleep all the time, there was nothing else for me to do.

Our people don't like to go to clubs. After working in the cotton fields, they're tired. They come home and there are six or seven children there, they have to cook the food and do the washing by hand, clean the house and look after their husbands, listen to the reproaches from their fathers-in-law and mothers-in-law. And do a whole load of other things as well. In short, they don't really have much time to amuse themselves. And so I didn't have anything to do. The East, as they say, is a "subtle business." I used to lock myself in the club, turn on the music, and dance on the stage alone. Completely alone!

After a while the exam session began. I went away to Tashkent and phoned Ikram from there. He said that he would come to see me.

I got a telegram from him. I met him at the airport, and we went to the hostel. We had a meal together, and then we talked and remembered. Then we went for a walk to the park. And he asked me to go to Turkmenia with him to meet his parents. I didn't agree: what was this all about? He said he had decided to marry me. I told him that in our parts we weren't allowed to show ourselves to the groom's parents and relatives before the wedding. He replied that his family was European and cultured: "Just say yes, I'll only introduce you to them." He tried to persuade me for so long that in the end I finally agreed.

I passed the exams and two days later we went to Turkmenia and arrived in Tashauz. We walked up to their house and rang the bell. The gate was opened by a beautiful woman with blue eyes, his mother. She said hello and hugged me. We went into the house. In the hall there was a man sitting at a table, my future father-in-law: a nice-looking man with curly hair and long eyelashes: no wonder his nickname was Pushkin, from the Russian word for "fluffy"—*pushisty*. He said hello to me as well.

Their lounge was very beautiful, there were large, expensive Turkmen carpets on the floor and the walls. There were fruits lying on a large crystal tray on the table: pomegranates, apples, tangerines, grapes. To this day I still remember the way Ikram's parents looked me over from head to foot. But I just looked at the fruit and wondered when they would go to bed.

Then my father-in-law said:

"She's come straight from the train, after all. Raya, show her the bathroom and everything else."

His mother showed me to the bathroom. While I was getting washed, it turned out that Ikram's father asked him when, where, and under what circumstances we had met, who I was and where I was from. It was a good thing we'd agreed in the train what to say if they asked.

Ikram went to get washed after me. And while he did, his father asked me questions. I told him everything just the way it was, apart from the intimate details, because I couldn't tell him about that. Finally Ikram's parents went to bed. As soon as they'd gone, I threw myself on the fruit and ate almost all of it in an instant. Afterward I felt ashamed of behaving like a ragamuffin. But what do you think—I was a student, I wasn't paid much, and before that, my mother had a lot of children, where would we get tangerines? I'd never even dreamed of having any.

Early in the morning Ikram's father said he wanted to invite all his relatives and consult with them about me, that is, tell them that his son had brought a girl home. He began phoning them all and arranging a meeting at eight o'clock in the evening. Ikram noticed that I was nervous and he reassured me:

"Just don't you worry, I'm with you, everything will be all right."

Aunty Raya made pilaf. At eight o'clock in the evening all the relatives came and we had supper together. The relatives looked me over from head to toe as well. One woman said:

"How can she do that—turn up here at the house before the wedding, if my daughters did that, I'd rip their heads off! Don't you have any parents?" she asked me.

I didn't answer. What could I say? I was in the wrong. Then another woman joined in:

"How shameless!"

But a third one answered them:

"Let's not make the situation any worse. Let's talk about what we're going to do now."

Ikram's father said to me:

"Daughter, you stay here for now, and Ikram's mother will go to your home in Uzbekistan to see your parents and tell them that you're here."

Then one of the women came up to me and said:

"Since you came here on your own two feet, there won't be any wedding! So don't even dream about it! What nerve."

After that attack I was really upset, and I wondered why I'd listened to Ikram and gone there . . .

But then I took a grip on myself and answered:

"I beg your pardon, of course, but in the first place Ikram brought me here to introduce me to his parents, and I'm not the one asking him to marry me. In the second place, my parents think that I'm still in Tashkent, at the exam session. In the third place, if I stay here without getting married, the rumors will spread in my village that I've run away from home, and because of me my younger sisters won't be able to get married, because people will blame me and say: 'If their sister ran away from home to God knows where, what can you expect from the younger sisters?' And so I had better go back to Tashkent. Pleased to meet you, good-bye." And I tried to leave.

Ikram's father stopped me and said to them:

"What did I ask you all to come here for? Let's decide what we're going to do."

The relatives said:

"You should ask your son what to do. He's the one who brought her into the house."

Then they all crowded round Ikram:

"Do you love her?"

He answered calmly:

"Yes, I love her, and she's the only one I'll marry."

Then one of the women said:

"All right, if that's how it is, it's fate. Now we have to go to the kishlak with her. We'll ask the neighbors there about her parents, who they are and what their daughter's like. If it turns out that everything is all right, we'll make a match and hold a wedding. If they say she's not from a respectable family, then we'll come back here. We don't need a bride like that. And you, my dear, don't stay here, go home. On Saturday we'll come to make the match."

In short, my first meeting with them ended with them coming to the conclusion that they would only hold a wedding if I turned out to be from a respectable family.

They gave me money for my journey, and I went home. When my parents saw me, they wondered where I could have come from. I told them I had passed the tests and the exams, that the exam session was over and everything was all right. After that there were no more questions.

*   *   *

The long-awaited Saturday arrived. I was waiting for the match-makers, but for some reason they were late. I waited in the morning, until dinner, then until supper. I was worried, I thought it was all over, they wouldn't come now. But just then a car stopped in front of our house. I was so happy I jumped up and down and shouted so everyone in the house could hear:

"They're here! They're here! Hooray!"

My brother looked at me in surprise and asked:

"Who's here?"

Then I realized what a mess I'd made and said I didn't know. I was frightened in case my parents found out that I hadn't just been in Tashkent at the exam session . . .

The matchmakers came into the house. The custom in our parts is that when the matchmakers come in, the girl has to hide. Even though I'd already seen them all, I followed the custom and hid in the room. My parents weren't home, they were at a wedding. We had to send my brother to get them. An hour later my mother and father arrived and saw strangers in their home. They introduced themselves to each other and began talking.

My father said:

"She's still studying."

The matchmakers answered:

"What of it, she can carry on with her studies after the wedding too. Let's hold the wedding soon, we'll do everything in two weeks."

"Why such a hurry? I'm not ready yet. I have to buy a few things, there's no chest, no cupboard, no carpet, no divan. I can't do everything in such a short time. And then, you know yourself—you probably have grown-up children too, you have daughters who are married and daughters-in-law—according to the rules you have to come another two or three times to discuss everything: the bride price, the expenses, and so on."

But they replied:

"We live very far away and we all have jobs, we don't have the time to come here again. If we lived nearby, that would be a different matter. And as for all the rest: the cupboard, the carpet, the divan, the money—that will be taken care of. We have all that at home."

My father said:

"I don't doubt that you have everything, but my daughter is not a widow, to be leaving the house with nothing. According to our custom—you must understand me—she has to leave the house with all these things, and everybody must see it, because everybody does that, those are our rituals."

The matchmakers agreed to bring everything, including the bride price. And they also said that Ikram loved me. It was a good thing they didn't give me away and say I'd been at their house. And it was good they didn't know that I danced! Or else there wouldn't have been any matchmaking.

Thirteen days later my wedding took place.

Just as they'd promised, the matchmakers brought everything: the trunk, the divan, the cupboard, four mattresses covered with expensive material, four cushions, two sheep, thirty-six liters of cottonseed oil, forty kilograms of rice, forty bread cakes, forty kilograms of apples, one crate of candy, two crates of vodka, two crates of champagne, two crates of lemonade, two seventy-five-kilogram sacks of flour, four different pieces of cotton cloth, each ten meters long, a suit for my father and one each for my brothers, an expensive shawl for my mother, and material for dresses for my sisters. And there were clothes and shoes for me too, four gold rings, a chain, earrings, and a bracelet.

A bride price had been paid for my mother in her time, too. They drove her and all her girlfriends on a tractor pushing along a trailer with all her dowry lying in it. The tractor rattled as it drove along—trrr-trrr-trrr!

The Story of How Weddings Are Celebrated in Our Parts

In general, in our parts a wedding is a complicated ritual. In the towns now everything is simpler, of course. But before, the customs used to be strictly observed, the way they still are in the kishlaks. The groom's parents used to bring the bride price: rice, flour, cottonseed oil, candy, the bride's clothes, pieces of cloth for dresses, satin, brocade, crepe de chine, shawls. They used to bring pieces of cloth for *kurpachkas* (padded mattress covers), for mattresses, cushions and blankets, quilts.

When my parents got married, there was no cotton wadding to stuff the cushions, the mattress, and the quilt. In their spare time the women all sat in their houses picking the bits out of the cotton and making wadding, even though it was forbidden, all the cotton had to be given to the state.

The old women from the kishlak came to sew the dowry for the bride. First they beat up the wadding with two sticks to make it fluffy. Then they laid out the material with the reverse side upward, spread the wadding over it evenly, covered it with cloth, and stitched it across. They sewed a blouse out of white cotton material for the first wedding night. After the work all the women were treated to a meal.

The father of the bride used to buy a decorated chest for the dowry from the craftsmen at the bazaar. When a bride is preparing for her wedding, the groom's parents come to the house to find out what is needed for the celebration. The bride must not show herself to the groom's parents, she sits in a different room at this time. If she needs something, she gets someone to tell the groom's parents about it. They brought my mother a plush coat as well (she wore it for twenty more years!) and black *maskhi* (the kind of boots you put galoshes on).

Before she goes away to someone else's home, the bride holds a party for her girlfriends. Two of her close friends go round the kishlak, inviting everybody. They come with presents: either little headscarves with lace sewn round the edges, or soap, or scent. The bride accepts the presents and hands them to a close female relative, who puts them all together in one place.

The girls sit on the floor in a room and talk. They talk to each other about their dreams, marriage, their work in the collective farm fields, and all sorts of other things. After a meal they dance. Then the bride brings the big bundle and unwraps it in the middle of the room. Everybody gathers round and looks at the presents from the groom's family and discusses the presents, saying if they like them or not. One says:

"When I have my wedding, I'll ask for that as well."

Another says:

"But I'd rather ask for this," and she points to something that is regarded as fashionable in the kishlak. It's not surprising that all the women in the kishlak dress the same, like incubator chickens.

The girls stay for the night. One of the bride's friends sprinkles henna into a deep cup, asks for a little bit of eau de cologne, and dilutes it with warm water. Then they wind cotton wool onto a matchstick and start writing the initials of the man they love on the backs or palms of their hands or on their breasts. They write: "I love you! You are my only one." Or: "Where are you, my beloved?" And they sit there until the morning, waiting until the henna dries.

The bride is prepared for her wedding night by a close female relative. This girl has to be beside the bride at all times. The bride heats water and washes her body, she shaves the hairs under her arms and below her stomach.

A special person prepares pilaf for dinner. The bride sits in the room with her friends. This is when the older women come in and bring the wedding dress. Then everyone else except the bride has to leave. The women say:

"Little daughter, it's time already, take off your clothes and put this on."

When she hears these words, the bride starts to cry and runs away into another room, the women follow her, saying:

"Don't cry, little daughter, it's the same fate for everyone."

Another says:

"Be glad that someone has taken you. Some have to sit and wait for their happiness."

They help her to take her clothes off and put the wedding dress on her. The girls weave the bride's hair into braids— sometimes two, sometimes forty, but never one. The women put an embroidered skullcap on the bride's head, cover her forehead with a special white headscarf, and say:

"Oh, Allah, now she will come out like the bright moon! Save her from sorrows!"

The reason for the headscarf is this: On the wedding night the bride and the groom sleep together, and then the groom demands that the bride must prove her virginity. Then the bride takes the white headscarf off and wipes herself with it. If the headscarf is stained red with blood, her virginity is proven.

After dressing the bride, they feed her to keep up her

strength. Although at that moment she is so excited that she doesn't want to eat at all.

The people sit in the house and wait for the bride to come out, then they set off to take her to the groom. At this time everyone is eating the pilaf.

When the bride appears, her girlfriends surround her, throw a big bedspread over her quickly, and lead her out into the street, where a crowd of people is waiting. Everybody asks the father to bless his daughter.

Then they take the bride to the groom.

They stop the car not far from the groom's house. One of the groom's relatives makes a small fire, and the car has to drive through it. This is an ancient custom from pagan times, now with automobiles instead of horses. And they won't let anybody cross the road in front of the car—that's a sign that there won't be any children.

They help the bride to walk, because she can't see anything under the bedspread. Someone from the groom's side stands at the door and speaks the names of his relatives. The bride has to bow in honor of each of them. After this ceremony they say to the bride:

"Step into the house with your right foot!"

And the bride steps across the threshold with her right foot. This custom is passed on from generation to generation.

After the wedding, if everything is all right in the house, they say:

"Good, the bride stepped into the house with her right foot!"

If something unpleasant happens, they reproach her and say:

"You stepped into the house with the wrong foot!"

I was married in the same way as all our women. This ritual is handed down with only small changes from one generation to another.

By midday on the day of the wedding, the older women had put my white dress on me and tied the white headscarf— the sign of virginity—on my head. They covered me with a big bedspread and told me to cry. But at that moment I couldn't cry, and that was all there was to it. My neighbor tugged on my arm and said:

"Cry, cry, or else people will talk—they'll say she's leaving her own home and didn't shed a tear."

"I can't cry," I answered.

She pinched me. "You fool, who's going to see, you fool! Just yell, that's all, at least pretend."

I had to pretend I was crying, although under the bedspread I was really happy that I was getting married.

Before I got into the car, my father blessed me. And then we set off in seven cars and one truck with the cupboard, the divan, and the carpets. We crossed the border and arrived in the town of Tashauz. They were waiting for us there. We slaughtered a sheep and held the wedding.

* * *

The guests didn't sleep that night. They were waiting for the result from us two. In the morning my husband had to demonstrate my virginity to them. That was when I started crying for real. My husband tried to calm me down. We both wondered how we could get out of this situation, what we could do. Suddenly Ikram said:

"That's it, I've got it! Bibish, don't you worry, everything's going to be all right. I'll be right back. You lie here and wait for me, all right?"

Ten minutes later he came back with a paper bundle. He locked the door from the inside and then unwrapped the newspaper, and I saw a piece of fresh meat. He took the white headscarf off my head and began rubbing the meat on it. It made a bloody stain.

Early in the morning all the relatives gathered in the yard. Ikram came out with the headscarf that he had rubbed the meat on and showed it to them. They praised him and said: Well done, well done. Then they all went home. Thank God, everything went off all right. Nobody suspected anything. So thanks to my husband I was saved, otherwise his family would have driven me out and sent me back to my village like a dog.

After the wedding, some of the relatives stayed to clean up the house and wash the dishes. They told me that when they were on the way to make my match, before they reached our house they asked people what I was like, was I married or not, whether I came from a good family or a bad one. Fortunately, almost everyone had said: "She's always studying," "Her father's a teacher, a simple, good man," and some had simply said: "How should we know what she's like?"

It was a good thing they didn't meet any bad people, the kind who like to spread rumors everywhere.

So now my eternal suffering was over, I thought, although I didn't know yet what was waiting in store for me.

But first I want to tell you about the house I found myself in after our poverty at home. Ikram's parents had a very big house, with every convenience. The yard was surrounded by a brick wall, and it had two terraces and a vegetable garden of five hundred square meters. There were various types of grapes growing in the garden. The early ones ripened in May and June, and the autumn ones were still good until November: they hung there in big bunches. A lot of vegetables and very beautiful flowers were growing there.

For the winter my father-in-law used to hang the grapes up in a special room, with the bunches a little distance away from each other so that the air could circulate. In winter the temperature in this room never changed. They stored the grapes there and ate them until the next harvest.

They used to store melons too. They made special nets out of reeds and put each melon in a separate one, then hung them up.

There were ten rooms in the house: a huge entrance hall, four bedrooms, a nursery, three drawing rooms, and a study with books. There was also a big kitchen and a corridor. The toilet, bathroom, and garage were in the yard. Their car was a Zhiguli. All the rooms had carpets lying on the floor and hanging on the walls and Romanian furniture.

I couldn't keep up with cleaning all the rooms, but on the weekends my mother-in-law helped me.

After the wedding my mother-in-law came into our room and said:

"Daughter, from tomorrow we'll go back to work. In our house there's always a routine: breakfast at eight fifteen, lunch at one fifteen, dinner at six fifteen. My husband likes cleanliness and order. We have a lot of guests. You must always be on time and try to be neat, do you understand?"

I only nodded in reply, because in our parts it is forbidden to talk to your mother-in-law and father-in-law for a whole year, for a whole year you can't say anything, only nod your head and explain yourself with gestures, as if you were deaf and dumb. That's the custom, all the young brides in our parts follow this rule. But since Ikram's mother was Russian, she didn't want me to walk around without saying anything all the time. She said with a smile:

"You can talk to me. In our home we don't have any little children to translate your gestures, so say what you want to say, otherwise you can go crazy saying nothing for a year."

And I used to talk to my mother-in-law, but not my father-in-law, for about a year and a half I observed the rule and said nothing to him.

The next morning I got up and brewed green tea for myself. We had breakfast together. While we were sitting at the table, my father-in-law took an apple, showed it to me, and said:

"Look, I'm holding an apple. It doesn't matter if it's big or small." He divided the apple into four parts with a knife. Then he gave one to each of us and said: "You always do the same thing, you mustn't think only of yourself. Whatever comes into your hands, share everything with the people close to you. I hope you understand now that we are one family."

My mother-in-law worked as a senior economist in a trading depot, and my father-in-law was the deputy head of a materials and equipment supply office. My husband worked as a welder and automobile mechanic, he didn't have a standard working day. As she went off to work, my mother-in-law said to me:

"Bibish, I tell you what: we'll be back from work for lunch, because we work nearby. You make us some thick rice pudding."

Then they both went off to work, and Ikram stayed with me.

I said to him:

"Do you happen to know how to make rice pudding with milk?"

"How should I know? You ought to have asked my mother."

"I'm shy."

"You've no need to be shy." And he went off to sleep.

And like a fool, I walked backward and forward between our room and the kitchen a hundred times. I thought that first you poured water into the pan, then put in the rice and added milk. I put the pan on the gas. I waited. Nothing was happening. I threw in a lot of salt. I turned the gas right up and the rice stuck and burned. I began to cry. It was already almost one o'clock. God only knew what it was I'd made.

I wanted to make tea and went out into the yard to throw out the old brew, and just then the gate opened and my father-in-law came in. Wearing a suit and tie and hat. When I saw him I was so nervous I caught the spout of the teapot on the door. While he was in the toilet I found some newspapers, wrapped the broken teapot in them, and threw it in the garbage, then quickly made the tea in something else. Before I got used to him coming home, I broke the spouts off seven teapots.

My mother-in-law came, looked at me, and asked:

"Why have you been crying, have you had a quarrel with Ikram?"

I didn't answer.

At one fifteen I put lunch on the table. My father-in-law ate one spoonful and said:

"Thank you, daughter, it's very good." And he immediately pushed his plate away. I tried it as well and found I'd oversalted it.

My mother-in-law realized everything, stood up, went into the kitchen, and three minutes later she brought him an omelette. As she was leaving to go back to work, she said:

"Bibish, let me write down the recipe for the simplest dish for you: meat broth."

She took a piece of paper and wrote: "Pour cold water into a saucepan and put the meat into it. When the water begins to boil, put in onions and carrots and add potatoes about half an hour later, or they will be overcooked."

"Take the recipe and make it for supper."

When they left to go to work, I started wandering round the rooms. They had a huge house, ten large rooms: you could get lost in it. Naturally—my father-in-law used to be the director of a brick factory. He built the house himself.

The furniture was good, there were seventeen expensive carpets and crystal, everything was clean and tidy. I checked the little cupboards and tried to sort out the postcards and some papers and documents. I cleaned the medicine cupboard and threw out the medicines that were no good because they were out of date. I remember my mother-in-law was annoyed after that and said to me:

"I can't find the addresses and the documents I want. Bibish, you shouldn't have touched them, they were lying in the same place for thirty years, and now I have to search to find them!"

As well as that, I found an entire crate of condensed milk and drank down a whole can—glug-glug-glug—straightaway. I wanted to open another can, but I stopped myself. I'd have plenty of time to do that. So I swallowed one can every day, and soon there wasn't a single can left in the crate. When my husband saw the empty crate, he laughed:

"It's good you drank it or else it would have just laid there, as if it was on exhibition."

But let's get back to the recipe.

As it got closer to six o'clock I started making the meat broth for dinner. I poured cold water into the saucepan, just as the recipe said. When the water started to boil, I put in the meat, and then the onion and carrot straightaway. I saw the scum had already stuck to the meat, it was terrible, oh, what was I supposed to do? I turned off the gas, poured out the boiled water together with the scum, and washed each piece of meat under the tap, but the scum was so stuck to the meat that it just wouldn't come off. In short, all the tasty, fatty water went down the drain. I'd spoiled everything again. I was really upset again and I cried. The time was already six o'clock. Ikram's parents came home from work. I laid the table. My mother-in-law immediately sensed that I'd done something wrong. She quickly boiled some potatoes and put them on the table.

The next morning, my mother-in-law was hurrying to get to work. As she was going, she left me a recipe for a sauce. This time I made the sauce exactly the way it said in the recipe. When it seemed to be ready and smelled good, all I still had to do was to salt it. There were lots of little boxes in the cupboard on the wall in the kitchen. Out of curiosity I opened every one of them. Tea, sugar, spices, and in one of them I saw a fine white powder. I thought: Oh, who would have thought salt could be as fine as that? I took a tablespoonful of the "fine salt" and put it in the cauldron. The sauce in the cauldron started to froth. I tried it and it tasted disgusting! If only you knew what I'd gone and done! That "fine salt" turned out to be household soda!

Without even waiting for my mother-in-law to arrive, I poured out all the sauce into the rubbish bucket and then began waiting, terrified, for the evening, when everybody would come back from work. I was thinking: Now they'll come home and scold me. Nothing was ready to eat, everything had gone into the garbage. But no, I was wrong, nobody scolded me because of that. When my mother-in-law came into the kitchen, I was so ashamed I almost fell through the floor and I cried again. She said:

"Something's happened again, why are you crying?"

Ikram answered her for me:

"Mom, it turns out she doesn't know how to cook at all, and that's why she's crying."

"Never mind," said my mother-in-law. "You've got your whole life ahead of you. You'll learn. To avoid all our wages just being thrown in the garbage every day, I'll do the cooking now, like before, Bibish, and you you're going to help me, all right?"

* * *

After that incident my mother-in-law always prepared more food for dinner in the evening and put what was left in the refrigerator so that lunch for the next day was ready.

And that was how she cooked for a whole twelve years, until we moved to Russia. My father-in-law used to reproach her for it:

"Who's the daughter-in-law in our house, you or her? Raya, you're really spoiling her!"

The relatives used to rebuke her too:

"All the housework should be done by the daughter-in-law, you paid her parents a bride price for her!"

But my mother-in-law never scolded me or tormented me the way mothers-in-law in my native parts do. The two of us got on very well and arguments happened only rarely, but you know yourself that always happens in a family: there are joys and sorrows—everything together. My mother-in-law mostly spoke Russian, and she spoke Uzbek with an accent.

During the first period of our life together, I noticed that my mother-in-law slept apart from her husband. I started wondering why. My parents had always slept together, but every evening Ikram's parents went to different rooms.

I asked Ikram:

"Why does your mother sleep separately from her husband? After all, she's still young."

"She's not well," Ikram replied briefly.

"What has she got?"

"I don't want to say. Ask her yourself."

"It seems awkward somehow."

"What's wrong with it? Ask, and you'll get to know each other better as well."

One day I finally plucked up my courage and asked my mother-in-law about her life. I made tea for when she came home (we used to drink green tea before a meal in order to stop ourselves feeling tired). We sat at the table in the huge kitchen.

"How is your work going?" I asked. "Is everything all right?"

"Everything's fine. I am working on a report."

I was tormented by curiosity. I gave her some tea and said:

"Mom, tell me about yourself."

She laughed:

"Are you interested?"

"Of course!"

"All right then. But it's a long story."

And she started telling me.

My Mother-in-Law's Story

My mother and father came from Russia, from the Ulyanovsk region. My mother didn't speak until she was nine. One day my mother's older sister grabbed a burning stick out of the stove, held it up to her mouth, and said:

"Come on, now, say 'mama-papa'!"

My mother was frightened and she shouted: "Mama! Papa!" and then hid under the bed. Her sister ran to their parents to tell them the little girl had said something. After that she began talking. But my mother finished only three grades of school.

She grew up and married a young man from her village. When they got married, someone jinxed them: they couldn't live with each other as husband and wife. Then they went to a healer. The healer advised them to go away from the village. And that's how my parents came to be in Uzbekistan. My father worked as an irrigator: he used to measure the level of the water in the Amudarya and its tributaries, and sail along the river in a boat. But later the people he worked for sent him to study. And soon my father was transferred to work in Turkmenia.

The first child they had was a boy, Boris. Once they had to travel through the sands on camels. It was very hot. The little boy caught dysentery and died. At the new place in Turkmenia, I was born. Then came my sister and my brother.

When the war started, my father went to the front. My mother was left alone with three children. She got work with the post office, delivering telegrams. She had to work even at night. There were a lot of death notices. My mother used to suffer for everyone who had been killed.

After that she moved to a different job—she used to spray small marshes with chemicals to kill mosquitoes that carried malaria. And she used to deliver quinine—the medicine for malaria—to people who were sick. Sometimes she took me with her. The collective farm people used to live in shelters made of branches. They didn't even have doors.

It was very difficult for my mother to feed us. She collected the last of her things—pieces of satin, plush, and cotton cloth —then she went round the villages and exchanged it all for a cow. Now we had milk.

When I started school my mother made me a bag in the shape of an envelope out of scraps of material. There weren't enough textbooks. To get something to write on, we used to go to the wastepaper depot and look for blank pages in the books. Sometimes we used to write on newspapers.

One day my mother got a letter from the front. They wrote that my father had been wounded in the collarbone and he was in the hospital. They hadn't been able to get the bullet out. My father was sent to the rear, to Chelyabinsk, to join a flying group. He served there until the end of the war and then came home.

Soon after that he was moved to the town of Kerki on the banks of the Amudarya. My mother didn't work, she looked after the house.

After I graduated from a seven-year Russian school, I went to study in Ashkhabad with several other girls. We traveled in train cars that carried cargo, because we didn't have any passenger trains back then.

When I finished my studies, I was assigned to the town of Tashauz.

During the times when I was young, there weren't any televisions or tape recorders. The young people used to go to the town park in the evening. There was a dance floor there, and an open-air movie theater.

So I used to go to the park too, with my friend Nina. She was my very best friend, we've been friends for more than fifty years.

It was spring, early March. The cherry and apricot trees were covered in snow-white flowers, the apple and peach trees were just beginning to put out pink blossoms. It was very beautiful.

At first Nina and I were going to go to the open-air movie theater, but then we heard the music from the dance floor, and went running over there. A brass band was playing. We really put our hearts into the dancing: the waltz, and the tango, and the foxtrot.

Then suddenly we saw some young men who lived on the same street as us. They were quarreling with someone. We went over, to prevent a fight, and persuaded them to walk home with us.

There was a young man about average height walking beside me. I hadn't met him before. He had a dark complexion and curly black hair. We walked along without speaking, then suddenly he said to me:

"Are you from round here? I haven't seen you before."

"I'm from the district, I haven't been here long."

"What's your name?"

"Raya."

"My name's Kadyr. Are you a student?"

"No, I've finished my studies. I work now."

We talked for a long time. I found out he was in the Soviet Army, he'd come there on vacation, and his leave ended the next day.

He stuck close beside me. And then he said in a very familiar tone:

"I've really taken a liking to you. Let's go to my place!"

I was indignant and I answered: "No!"

I had to stay with my friend for the night so that Kadyr wouldn't find out where I lived. I said good-bye to Kadyr in front of her house, and we left him. He started banging on the door to be let in. But we didn't react.

Early in the morning I had to go to work. I opened the door and saw Kadyr lying on the doorstep! He got up straightaway and said:

"Forgive me, please, but I couldn't go away after I saw your blue eyes and light brown hair. I want to be beside you all the time."

He walked me to work and left. After that I didn't see him for a long time.

Time went by and I worked and helped my mother with the housework. One day my younger sister came back from the park and said:

126

"Listen, Raya, there was a young man asking about you at the dance."

"Who's that?" I asked, surprised.

"How should I know?"

"But what does he look like?"

"He's medium height, with curly hair, very attractive-looking, actually."

I realized who she was talking about and thought:

So, Kadyr has come back from the army. The next weekend I went to the park with my girlfriends to go dancing. When we got there, we sat down on some benches. The music started to play. Everybody went off in pairs to dance, and I was left sitting there. Suddenly I saw a familiar face among the dancers: it was Kadyr dancing with some girl. And then our eyes met. He left the girl in the middle of the dance floor and came over to me, took hold of my hands, and asked me to dance.

Our love began from that day.

We used to meet often and go swimming with our friends or go out into the country. Kadyr was very jealous. He didn't like it if any of the young men came near me. Sometimes it ended in a fight. Because of his hot temper we used to have quarrels too. But I put up with it all and forgave it all because I loved him very much.

And then we decided to get married. But my parents were against it. They wanted me to marry a Russian.

My love flared up more brightly with every day, and I

decided to leave home and go to Kadyr. And so I went straight from our latest date to his house.

As well as Kadyr's mother and father, his half brothers and sisters lived with the family.

Kadyr's mother was called Nazira. She came from Khiva. Her father was a very rich man, and he had married his daughter into a rich family too. She had children—a son and a daughter. But just at that time Stalin's campaign against *kulaks*, the landowners, began. Nazira's father and her husband were exiled to Siberia, and all their wealth was confiscated. Nazira was left alone with two children. Some time later Nazira's father came back from exile and came straight to Turkmenia, without calling at his home in Khiva—he was afraid they would take him again.

He was very concerned about the fate of his daughter and grandchildren. Soon after that he married her off again to a craftsman from Tashauz (he made traditional metal-bound trunks). Nazira had a lot of children by her new husband, but only three of them survived. Kadyr's stepfather regarded him as his own son, and he passed on his trade to him and his half brother.

Although I was a Russian-speaker, I was accepted in the house and respected.

At that time Kadyr graduated from teacher training college and went away to work where he was assigned, in Kunya-Urganch, as a teacher of Russian. But I stayed with his parents, since I was pregnant. He only had to work there for a year, so I decided not to go.

The first child we had was a daughter. Then came Ikram, your future husband. Then our youngest son.

Our financial situation improved. Kadyr began to be appointed to various high positions. Of course, he joined the Party. His character gradually began to change, but I didn't notice that. Or rather, I didn't want to notice.

There was nothing that we were short of. People in the districts that he supervised used to send us food and even sheep.

Every year we went to resorts. Although we always went separately. Once I went to a sanatorium in Sochi. I saw that all the women were going to the gynecologist for a checkup, and I decided to go and get myself checked too. And the doctor said to me:

"You have to be examined in the cancer clinic."

"What for?" I was surprised.

"Nothing to worry about, just for prophylactic purposes," she reassured me. But afterward it turned out she'd said that only women from Central Asia were so badly neglected.

I came back home and told my husband everything. We were both forty then.

"Let's go to Ashkhabad tomorrow, they'll cure you there, and everything will be all right," he said.

The doctors at the hospital in Ashkhabad wouldn't let me leave, they said I had to stay.

Kadyr bought me everything I needed: slippers, towels, a dressing gown, a kettle, a mug. He said:

"You get well. I'll phone you often."

They started giving me radiation treatment immediately. I didn't get out of bed for three months. And all the time I was thinking about the children and what would happen to them if I died. Sometimes I cried.

At first Kadyr used to phone, then it was less and less often. He said he was very busy at work.

I found out afterward what happened when Kadyr came back home from Ashkhabad. When he got back, he phoned his relatives and his sisters and told them his wife was in a cancer clinic.

They told him:

"Then that's the end, your wife won't come back alive."

Others said:

"It's a terrible illness. You've been unlucky, Kadyr."

And his sister said:

"See, if you'd married an Uzbek woman, the whole house would have been made of gold."

In short, everyone expressed their own opinion. Kadyr didn't say anything in reply, he just listened. After a while Kadyr's sisters came to him and began trying to persuade him:

"Kadyr-aga, we're suffering so much for you! Can we tell you some news?"

"What news is that?"

"We'll tell you, but you promise you won't be angry."

"Of course I won't be angry with you, now tell me."

"Kadyr-aga, we thought and thought, and we decided that you mustn't be left all alone with little children. Only Allah knows if your wife will get well or not. So we looked for a bride for you and found a very good woman. She knows about you from hearsay and is willing to meet you. We want you to get to know her."

Kadyr hadn't been expecting a suggestion like that, and he got really angry:

"Don't talk such nonsense! My wife is still alive. How could you say something like that? I won't listen to you!"

But they carried on pressing their point:

"Kadyr-aga! We'll all leave this world for the next, what's to be done! And not many people manage to beat cancer. It's such a terrible disease. Think about the children!"

Kadyr finally gave way to their persuasion and met the woman. They probably liked each other. They started something like an affair. He didn't come to Ashkhabad, and he only phoned me occasionally. Kadyr's sisters began gradually preparing for the wedding. They even named a possible day.

That was when Kadyr stopped phoning me completely.

Then after three months, with God's help, I was still alive. And I came home.

When they discharged me from the hospital, the doctors had warned me that I mustn't sleep with my husband. If I didn't do as they said, I could die.

* * *

Kadyr and his sisters' jaws dropped, they were so astonished, but they didn't say anything to me. And so my husband's wedding never happened!

But he put the question point-blank:

"Raya, please forgive me, of course, but I'm still young, I want to live a normal life, I want to sleep with you, but you can't. What am I to do? Carry on living like this until I die?"

I answered my husband:

"Kadyr, I understand you, you're still young. The only thing I ask of you, please Kadyr, for the sake of the children, don't throw me out of the house!"

Kadyr agreed not to divorce me, but on one condition— that I wouldn't try to stop him seeing other women on the side.

I agreed. I was an invalid, where could I go with three children? My parents were poor, and I was so weak, my mother used to come to help me. I didn't go back to work for a long time.

Kadyr used to come home when he wanted. He had a car and a driver from his job. And he had a car of his own. But he was still a family man: he did repairs at home, he brought the groceries, he made sure we didn't lack for anything. At night he kissed me and went to his own room, and I went to mine.

After a while we started getting strange phone calls. Different women used to call and abuse me:

"Hey you, leave Kadyr, I want to live with him!"

Or:

"You useless creature, I'm going to sleep with your husband!"

They tried to insult me and humiliate me any way they could, but I kept quiet and didn't say anything to Kadyr about these calls. I swallowed everything.

Kadyr was a Party member, and by local standards we still didn't have a very rich life. But he built houses for many of his mistresses, and many women exploited him (when he was the director of the brick factory). And he was very generous to his relatives too.

I can't say he's a bad man or a good one. If not for my illness, we'd have had a perfectly normal life.

What's to be done, Bibish? It's just my fate!

That was how she ended her story. I thought: How much women have to put up with!

And here's something I can add to this story. When my father-in-law fell ill with cancer, Raya nursed him devotedly. Nobody else wanted him then. And so he died in her arms.

I am grateful to my mother-in-law, she taught me a lot: how to deal with people, always to be amicable, not to envy anyone, to treat my illnesses with folk medicine, to dress with taste—otherwise I used to go about dressed gaudily all the time, like a set of traffic lights—how to talk to everybody in the right way, how to receive guests . . . I thank God that I have such a good mother-in-law. I always call her Mom.

But let's get back to my marriage. One day Ikram and I went to the bazaar together. They had a very big collective farm market, and a merchandise market beside it. Ikram wanted to show me all this. At the end, we went in to buy some fruit. There was everything, anything you could want, and all cheaper than in Russia. And I had a certain amount of my own money: my husband gave me it, and at the wedding people had thrown money onto my head too. So now I decided to spend some of it. Just then Ikram stopped to talk to someone and I went on among the fruit stalls. I walked along, looking for the cheapest apples and pomegranates, which meant they would be the worst too. I bought in a hurry, I don't remember how much, probably about three kilograms. It was the first time I bought anything as a wife. And then Ikram came up to me and asked:

"Well, my dear, what have you bought? Let's see what tasty things you have in your bag." He opened the bag, looked in, and was upset straightaway: "Why did you buy such rotten ones? Give me the bag, so my parents won't see, or else they say: 'Have you been digging in the garbage heap?'" He took the bag from me and threw all the fruit onto the garbage heap. Then he came up to me and said: "There's an old saying, 'The miser pays twice over.' So always buy only good fruit and good vegetables, that's no way to live, eating things that are rotten and smell bad."

I was very upset that he'd thrown out the fruit, because for as long as I could remember, in my childhood and my youth, I had eaten only cheap, half-rotten fruit like that. After all, my father hadn't been able to feed us properly. There were nine children, how could all of us be fed with expensive fruit? And what about clothes? How much money was my father supposed to have? After all he was the only one in the family with a job.

Ikram bought new fruit—good fruit, large and not rotten— and I felt very awkward. And then we went back home from the collective farm market.

After that I got so used to eating pomegranates that Ikram used to buy them for me by the sackful.

One day the relatives asked my father-in-law:

"Well, how's your daughter-in-law, is she getting used to city life? Are you pleased with her, or is she tricky and disobedient? Or perhaps bad-mannered? What's your opinion of her?"

"She's getting used to things, and we're getting used to her. There are no complaints so far, everything's all right. The only thing is, she eats an awful lot of pomegranates, we have to buy them by the sackful"—he laughed—"so if it goes on at this rate, our pay won't be enough. Well, let her eat them and enjoy them, she's welcome!"

And when he said that, everybody laughed.

* * *

We all got on very well together. They found me a job in an Uzbek school as a teacher in the elementary classes. My father-in-law was always saying:

"If only she could speak Russian, I could get her a job as a teaching methods specialist in the kindergarten. It's a shame she can't talk to anyone in Russian."

At home they spoke to each other in Russian and only sometimes in Uzbek—that was when the father's relatives came. And all the time I just listened to them and nodded my head.

One day we were sitting at the table—Ikram, his mother, and me—and just as I was saying something quickly, I don't remember what, Ikram stopped me and said in Russian:

"Don't rush!"

I stopped talking. I wanted to show that I'd understood. After a while I got up, went into the lounge, and found the Russian–Uzbek dictionary on the shelf. I wondered what "dontrush" meant. I looked right through the entire dictionary and couldn't find the word "dontrush" anywhere. It turned out to be a phrase!

Another time my husband and I were lying in bed dreaming, and he said in Russian:

"One day the two of us will buy a hut!"

I didn't know the word "hut," so I went to look for it in the dictionary again, and didn't find it anywhere. It turned out that "hut" was a Ukrainian word! I almost went crazy trying to find it! Only God knows how much I suffered to study the Russian language. And I promised myself: If I have children, to make life easier for them, I'll put them in a special Russian school.

A year went by. I went to Tashkent twice for the exam sessions and visited my parents several times. My mother-in-law gave them a new television. Before that they only had an old Snezhok television. When my father brought it home in the late sixties, I remember our neighbors and friends came to have a look at it, because not all of them had televisions.

And so a year went by after the wedding. My mother-in-law was worried all the time that I hadn't got pregnant, and my husband seemed to have lost hope that I would ever give him a child. Finally my mother-in-law took me to a gynecologist and I was treated for a long time. After the treatment I got pregnant. When they found out at home that I was finally pregnant, they wouldn't let me work at all, in case I might have a miscarriage. They were concerned about me all the time, they said: "Don't you get up, we'll do it. And they said: "You mustn't get excited, you mustn't lift anything, rest!" While I was pregnant I swelled up for some reason, I don't know why, maybe it was my kidneys, or because I used to sit in front of the television without moving.

One funny thing happened to me to do with that television. Basically, during the nine months when I was pregnant, I became like a real roly-poly. I was always sitting or lying on the divan and watching the television. One day the presenter on the Uzbek channel announced:

"Dear viewers! If you can see me, stop whatever you are doing and listen to this announcement. Here on the table there are flowers in a vase. Let me tell you that these flowers have been irradiated with Kashpirovsky's rays. Come closer to the screen."

I just barely managed to get up and move closer to the television.

The presenter said:

"Well now, viewers, I hope you have all moved closer to the screen, have you?"

I answered the announcer:

"Yes!"

The presenter went on:

"Even though these flowers are on the television, they are going to influence you. Sick people get well, and healthy people feel even better. So if you have moved closer to the screen, sniff the flowers."

So I began sniffing the screen. The presenter said:

"Well now, can you smell that scent, it smells like spring, doesn't it?"

I sniffed and sniffed at the television, then said to the screen:

"Yes, it does."

The presenter said:

"If you have taken a good sniff and followed the whole procedure, well done. And now I'd like to wish you a happy April Fools' Day, it was a joke, all the best, good-bye!"

I sat there on the floor completely confused. Just then my mother-in-law came into the room and asked:

"Why have you gone so close to the television? It's bad for you!"

Then I told her what had happened. How she laughed! And she said:

"We keep telling you: don't get up, don't move, rest, and you've just been really heroic and walked as far as the television!"

Exactly nine months went by. I was worried all the time in case the child would be born on the thirteenth day of the month. Because I was born on January 13, on New Year's Day in the old style, and I'd known nothing but suffering in life. It was already April 12, and I was walking around saying to myself: I mustn't give birth on the thirteenth. Evening came, it was about eight o'clock, and I had one little pain in my stomach, then it instantly disappeared. But I decided: This is it, I'm having the child! I alarmed everyone in the house. My husband immediately took me and a female neighbor to the maternity home in his car. They brought me to the reception area and a nurse was there.

She asked:

"When did it start?"

I said:

"What?"

"The contractions—why, is this your first time, then?"

"Yes."

"Right then, lie down and we'll check."

She checked me and said:

"My girl, your womb's only just opened a little bit, a finger's width. Why did you come so early?"

"I thought I was having the baby."

She laughed, called my husband into the corridor, and told him:

"Her contractions are still weak, take her back home, or she'll suffer here for a long time yet. Go, go home."

I refused to go home.

"I won't go."

"Go home, my girl, or they might give you cesarean section."

"I won't go home," I said, and began to cry.

"Why? It's still too soon for you to give birth, he can bring you when you have serious contractions."

"How will I be able to look my father-in-law in the eye, if I come back from the maternity home without having a child! What will he say?" How naive I was.

They barely managed to calm me down on the way back. When we got home, I felt so ashamed I went into my room as quickly as I could. My father-in-law rushed in from the lounge:

"What's wrong, why did you come back?"

He really was surprised to see me. The neighbor explained to him that I would have to go to the maternity home again. The women began reassuring me. All night long I tormented myself, and then that thirteenth day of the month came.

When we were going to the maternity home, my husband said to me:

"Do you hear me, have a son, only a son! If it's a girl, I won't pick you up from the maternity home!"

There was another nurse on duty when we arrived. She took me to the ward. I asked her:

"Can I put off the birth until the fourteenth?"

She laughed:

"No, my dear, it's time for you to give birth."

In the ward I screamed for all I was worth. One woman came running up to me:

"Hold on, hold on, the first time's always like that—look, I've just had twins." And she stroked my back.

The pain was terrible. I didn't know what to do with myself, I went out into the corridor and shouted:

"Why did I ever sleep with you, I'll never sleep with you again, never!" (That was about my husband.)

* * *

The doctors decided to give me a cesarean. My father-in-law didn't agree, and he said:

"She's young, let her give birth herself."

His word was law.

The agonizing contractions lasted exactly twenty-two hours.

When the time came for me to give birth, they put me on the chair, and the doctor kept repeating:

"Come on, push, you'll have the child now."

I was so anxious I kept saying:

"What is it, a boy or a girl?"

The doctor said:

"To find out which it is, first you have to have the child! Come on now, push!"

For us in the East it's very important for the first child to be a son, a man. I thought that if it was a girl, my husband really wouldn't collect me from the maternity home. Afterward I realized it was a joke, and they only keep you in the maternity home for six or seven days.

And so I had my first son, Aibek, on April 13 after all.

A week later I came back from the maternity home, and my father-in-law congratulated me.

"This time you gave birth, then?" he laughed.

After my son was born I had to go to Tashkent almost straightaway for the final state exams.

My mother-in-law said:

"Ikram and his father can stay at home, and I'll go with you. You can take the exams, and I'll stay with my grandson, all right?"

We set off with the little baby, he was only twenty days old.

In Tashkent we stayed with a girl student in my year. I took the exams one after another. My mother-in-law and my child were always there, close to me.

By the way, my little son was a great help to me with the exams. Do you wonder how?

This is what I asked the other students in my year to do when they were standing in line for the exam in the corridor:

"I'll go in, take a question ticket, and you immediately call out: 'I beg your pardon! Siddikova's baby is crying out here.' So then I'll come out, show you the ticket, and you write me a crib. Then I'll go in, and as soon as you've written the answer, call me again, I'll take the crib and go back in and answer the question."

That was how I passed the first exam.

I breast-fed my child regularly, and everything was all right. At the last exam I was standing in the corridor with my child in my arms, and as always my mother-in-law was close by.

Then suddenly my stomach started hurting really badly. My mother-in-law got angry and said:

"Of course it will hurt, because you go around with nothing on. You ought to have dressed warmly, you've only just given birth. And you're wearing nothing but your panties!"

My stomach hurt so badly that I couldn't go into the auditorium. I went back with my mother-in-law and my baby to the apartment we'd rented for the exams. We put the baby on the bed. My pain kept on as bad as ever. My mother-in-law went into the kitchen, warmed up some cottonseed oil, then came up to me, lifted up my dress, and poured the hot oil onto my navel.

"Your bowels are probably inflamed."

After that I simply couldn't bear it, I almost fainted from the pain.

My mother-in-law took fright and dialed 03 for the ambulance. The ambulance came, but they couldn't tell what was wrong, and they took me to a maternity home, because I'd recently given birth. At the maternity home, they kept me in reception for a long time and then said: "It's not our kind of problem, you have to take her to the surgical department in the republican hospital." Time passed while they were taking me there. But it turned out there wasn't any time to lose. In the surgical department they said: "Acute phlegmonic appendicitis. Peritonitis." It was almost too late to operate on me.

* * *

My baby and my mother-in-law had always been there beside me, everywhere I went. But now they took me into the operating theater, and my child was left without any breast milk. He was left out in the yard of the hospital with my mother-in-law.

Afterward my mother-in-law told me what happened to them.

She sat on a bench in the yard until eleven o'clock in the evening. They asked her: "What are you doing here so late?" She answered:

"I don't know where I should go. They've just operated on my daughter-in-law, and her baby has no milk."

My poor little boy was hungry, he kept looking for a nipple and crying all the time.

The doctors said:

"Where are you staying, tell us and we'll take you home."

But it was the first time my mother-in-law had been in Tashkent, she didn't know how to explain, and so she answered:

"My daughter-in-law's a student at the Institute of Culture, take me to the institute, then I'll be able to get my bearings and find my house. If it's not too much trouble, please take me to the institute."

They took her where she asked. From there she found her bearings and walked to the place where we were staying, with the baby in her arms.

*   *   *

My son wouldn't stop crying. Naturally, he was hungry and wet, because while they were waiting at the hospital they'd run out of diapers. My mother-in-law picked the baby up again and set off round the apartments. She knocked on doors and asked for something for the child: "Please give me some milk, even some dried milk for the little baby." Some people didn't even open their door, others said they didn't have any milk. She was tired from walking, and the baby kept screaming all the time. My mother-in-law kept on and on walking and finally she found some dried milk, given to her by a woman, but even then it was out of date. She had to risk it, what else could she do? She came home, mixed the powder with water, and fed the child from a bottle. Early in the morning she got up, picked up the child again, and went to the grocery store. She brought back some milk in a jar and then fed the child with that.

After that she phoned Turkmenia and told them what had happened. Ikram immediately left for Tashkent. My mother-in-law sat in the apartment with the child, and my husband came to see me in the hospital every day and brought me food and fruit.

They wouldn't let me feed my son or even see him, because when my appendix burst the pus and the infection had spread right through my body. I was in the hospital for exactly a month. And I was very worried that I hadn't managed to take the final state exam. The doctors said that in a case like this the teacher or the exam commission from the institute ought to come to the hospital themselves. But alas, no one came. I started crying and asking the doctors to let me go, I thought I might still be able to take the exam with the other students. The doctors said:

"It's too risky, the stitches could come open!"

I explained to them that I'd been studying for five years, and only the last exam was left and my five years would simply be wasted, and after the exam I'd get my diploma. "Please, let me go," I begged them.

Then they took me to the institute in an ambulance. I climbed out of the ambulance with a stick, after that they wouldn't allow me to walk any further, because the exam was on the third floor—I couldn't have walked up there anyway. They asked the exam commission to look out the window to make sure I had really turned up. Of course they looked out the window and saw I could hardly walk. And they explained to them that my appendix had burst and I had a child only one month old, a suckling babe to look after. They looked at my earlier marks and decided to give me my final mark without taking the exam. And that was how I graduated from the institute.

After a month I was discharged, and I went back to Turkmenia with my husband, my child, and my mother-in-law. At home my father-in-law and his relatives were waiting for us. They celebrated my graduation from the institute and the fact that I was alive and well. They admired my son.

But a week later I fell ill again—this time one of my kidneys failed. They took me to the hospital in an ambulance again, and I had a high temperature for a week. And I couldn't piss either, my bladder was inflamed.

I was in the urology ward for two and a half months. And again they wouldn't let me see my son. When I was discharged from the hospital, he was three and a half months old. Because of all my illnesses I hadn't been feeding him, and I was very worried.

When I came back home my mother-in-law immediately told me:

"He's mine now. If you want a child, have another one."

As soon as my mother-in-law told me to have a child, I got pregnant. Then my father-in-law suddenly fell ill, and the diagnosis was lung cancer. A few months later he died.

My mother-in-law sent me to the neighbors so that my son wouldn't be frightened during the funeral. He was exactly one year old, and I was almost eight months pregnant.

When they didn't see me at the funeral, my father-in-law's relatives came looking for me at the neighbors' house and began scolding me:

"Our brother slaved for you all, just for you, and you're hiding. What will people say? That his daughter-in-law wasn't at the service and she didn't cry! Come on now, leave the child here, let's go quickly, they're about to take him to the cemetery! You have to cry with us."

My mother-in-law didn't say anything, she couldn't contradict the relatives. I had to go with them. I walked into the room where the coffin was standing. Everyone there was weeping and keening and waving their arms around: "Why have you left us?," "How are we going to live without you?," "Oh, my sweet one!," "Oh my darling!" That was the way they showed their grief. But there wasn't a single tear in my eyes, even though I felt very sorry for him—he was only fifty-seven.

The relatives all looked at me reproachfully, and I had to think of something. I went through into the kitchen and took a knife and a couple of onions. There were a lot of people outside in the yard. I went into the bathroom without being noticed and started cleaning the onions with the knife. Then I rubbed them on my eyelids, my face, and my nose to make the tears appear. A few seconds later the tears started running from my eyes. Perfectly genuine tears! After that I simply couldn't stop them.

I went back to the relatives. I really was crying now, although not so much from grief as the bitter onions. But they still didn't think that was enough, they wanted me to throw myself about and shout—in short, to have an ecstatic fit. Like the other women. Just then one of our neighbors, a woman, came up to me and said:

"Get out of here. With a big belly like that you can't stay here, go, go!"

I shook my head:

"No, the relatives won't let me."

Then she went up to my mother-in-law and persuaded her to let me go until they took the coffin away. It was only then that my mother-in-law allowed me to go. What could she do? She was dependent on her husband's relatives, too.

A month and a half after my father-in-law died, my second son, Nadirbek, was born. How I wanted to avoid the thirteenth day of the month! But by ill luck I gave birth to my second son on the thirteenth. I was born on the thirteenth, my first son was born on the thirteenth, and my second son was born on the thirteenth! When I received my Turkmenian passport, it was issued on the thirteenth as well. It was a good thing that at least the months were different.

My first son, Aibek, is like my father-in-law: thin, with curly hair and a dark complexion. My second son took after my mother-in-law—he has fair skin, only his eyes are black and his eyelashes are very thick and long. The women I know say:

"Just for those eyelashes you want to have a little girl and give her to him, he's so handsome."

My first son is bright, but careless, he forgets everything: he leaves his school shoes, his jacket, and his cap at school.

He loves computers, and we don't have one. My second son is seriously interested in judo and sambo. He is very tidy and loves order.

The years went by, and how they passed only God knows. The children grew. My mother-in-law put them in a kindergarten, in a Russian group. After that they went to the Russian school and to the music school as well, they learned to play the piano. We bought them a piano, and they were good students. From childhood on they have spoken only Russian. They don't know their own language. When my older son was six, he came home from kindergarten and said:

"Mom, I'm getting married!"

"Who to?" I laughed.

"To a Russian girl, I don't want your ignorant Chukchas, I'll only marry a Russian girl."

That was the announcement he made when he was six.

I won't drag it out any longer, I'll write about our move to Russia. That's an amusing story too, in its own way. I think you'll be interested to know how people who have come from the former USSR survive in Russia.

My husband's grandmother was from Russia. She was born in 1908 in the Ulyanovsk region. Then it was the Simbirsk province. I've already told you about how they ended up in

Turkmenia. So then in 1999, thanks to my husband's Russian grandmother, we acquired Russian citizenship. And so my dream of living in Russia came true.

At first I went with a friend of mine, Lena—she's Russian—to the Kuybyshev region: her parents lived there, and she wanted to celebrate the New Year 2000 with them.

Before we went on reconnaissance to Russia, our neighbors and friends and my mother-in-law gave us the addresses of people they knew and said:

"Just in case you have nowhere to spend the night, or if anything happens—here are their addresses, stay with them and tell them 'your friends sent us here,' give them our greetings and a note."

There were enough addresses, a lot of them: Saratov, the Ulyanovsk region, Leningrad (my friend Anna Petrovna), Kaluga (my husband's brother lived there), another town in the central region of Russia (my mother-in-law's nephew Ravil lived there), and there were a lot of other addresses as well.

We set off on our journey in winter, in late December. We went on the Dushanbe–Moscow train. I was carrying a certificate that said I was a citizen of the Russian Federation, so on the way no one stopped or bothered me.

We decided to make our first stop in Saratov. We had to make up the cost of the tickets somehow, and we'd taken cotton things with us—T-shirts, panties, tracksuit pants, children's things, bedsheets, a lot of pairs of socks—so we could sell them on the way. And we also took ten cans of food each, and five kilograms of meat (beef), five lemons, dried apricots, walnuts, ten bread cakes, three kilograms of our national candy, peanuts, two kilograms of tea, and Iranian socks—presents for the people we were going to stay with.

So there we were in Saratov. And I had an address—a woman neighbor had given me it and said: "If you're in Saratov, you must go to see my friends." And I remember she gave me two jars of apricot jam for them as well.

At the station they told us we had to travel another thirty kilometers by bus. We had so many bags! We barely managed to drag them to the bus. We rode along and asked people the way, and they told us what was where. It was amazing: it's true what they say—you can find your way anywhere if you ask.

And so we arrived. My friend stayed at the bus station, and I went on to look for the address—the street and the house.

It was already evening, December, and very cold. I found the apartment and rang the bell. A woman asked from inside, without opening the door:

"Who's there?"

I asked her to open up. A large, tall, healthy elderly woman opened the door and said to me rudely:

"What do you want, wandering around here, I'm fed up with all these people! I haven't got anything, give one something, and another appears. Go away!" and she slammed the door.

I was taken aback. I don't know who she took me for, probably a gypsy woman. What could I do now? It was cold outside, it was night already, we didn't know anybody else there, where could we go? That address had been our only hope. I rang again, she opened the door again:

"If you don't go away, I'll call the militia this very moment."

"Your comrade sent me . . ." And before I could finish, she answered sharply: "The Tambov wolf is your comrade!" and slammed the door again.

I finally realized I had to give her the note from my neighbor. I rang, but no one answered anymore. My patience gave out too—I was frozen, after all, it was cold in the hallway too. I started hammering on the door with my hands. The moment she opened the door, and then her mouth, I handed her the note. She was surprised, she took the note and started reading it. After that—"Oi-oi-oi!"—she started apologizing and invited me into her home straightaway.

I told her I wasn't on my own. And I explained everything. She took her sled to help collect my friend and the things. My poor friend was standing at the bus stop, thinking I'd disappeared forever. When she saw me, she shouted out:

"Why did you take so long, I almost froze out in the cold!"

She said hello to the woman, and we went back to her home. At home there was another woman. They were Aunty Zoya and Aunty Klava, sisters. They used to live in Turkmenia too and they worked with my neighbor. They put the water on for tea straightaway, and we took out all the food and gave it to them. And we gave them the presents. Aunty Klava took all the food and put it away in the refrigerator.

We told them what our life was like back at home, and we also said we were going to sell our goods and go to the Kuybyshev region to see my friend's parents and celebrate the New Year 2000.

They said:

"We'll help you, we'll give you a folding bed to make it easier to sell your things. In the morning we'll go with you to the place where our dealers trade, and we'll stand there with you for a while, so they don't squeeze you out. After all, you're strangers to them, and you could be competitors."

In the morning we got up early. They went with us, showed us the place, and we started selling. Things didn't go well for my friend Lena, because she'd never traded before, she worked as a senior nurse in a drug addiction clinic. Anyway, I helped her to trade.

We came back to the apartment in the evening. Aunty Zoya and Aunty Klava were waiting for us, they asked how things were going. We said all right. After a whole day outside we were very hungry. And then the aunties said:

"We're on a diet, we don't eat much. Here's some mashed pumpkin for your supper."

And they had a dog, a collie—he was called Count—and a very beautiful cat as well. They poured the mashed pumpkin into plates for them, and some for us too. We were hungry and we didn't refuse, we agreed to eat it. And the food we'd brought—the meat, the fruit, and everything else—was lying in the refrigerator. We didn't dare open the refrigerator. They'd obviously decided that we'd brought them this food as a present as well. But we'd given them the Iranian socks!

And so every day we got up like that in the morning, and the women went on lying in their room. And we went off to trade without any breakfast. When we got back they were sitting there well fed. They just told us that they were on a diet, but in fact when we left they ate quick-quick-quick. And when we came back hungry, they were "on a diet." For a whole week Aunty Zoya and Aunty Klava fed us on that mashed pumpkin—crap for dogs. We had to eat it, we were out in the frost all day, on our feet! It was a good thing our packs were a bit smaller now, we had no strength left to carry them. When my friend Lena couldn't stand it anymore, she said:

"I can't bear to look at that mashed pumpkin anymore, the very sight of it makes me sick. I've had enough! Tonight, when they're asleep, we're going to open the refrigerator and have at least one decent meal. I'm already missing our bread cakes. Dammit, there are ten of them in the refrigerator, and plenty of meat as well. There were so many kilograms left after the train! No matter what, tonight we're getting up and eating. Bibish, just you try to say no, and I'll show you!"

So that night, when the sisters went to bed, we got up quietly and went into the kitchen. We put the kettle on for tea: so as not to choke on the meat and bread cakes, we had to drink something with them, you understand. We quietly opened the refrigerator, took the meat and bread cakes out, and began eating as quick as we could. If not for the tea, we really would have choked. Suddenly the door opened, and Aunty Klava came into the kitchen:

"What are you doing here in the middle of the night, eh?"

We sat there and said nothing. It was a good thing we'd already swallowed everything and tidied up after ourselves, or it would have been really unpleasant. We went to bed and giggled for a long time under the blankets because we'd managed to fool the "dieters," though we'd almost turned into dogs ourselves from that mashed pumpkin.

Ten days later our bags were empty, and we left for the Kuybyshev region to see Lena's parents. Lena sent them a telegram so that they would meet us. From the station we traveled another eighty kilometers or so. We finally reached the house, a brick cottage. While Lena's mom made dinner, we got washed.

Her parents had lived in Turkmenia too, thirty or forty years earlier. They had been officials. After the collapse of the USSR people started forcing them out because they were Russian. And so in 1992 they moved to Russia. In his new job her father worked as some kind of official again, but her mother had retired a long time ago.

Of course, I was living in someone else's home, so I couldn't feel at ease. We sat there having dinner and Lena felt fine, but I felt out of place, because her mother was fidgeting and fussing all the time, wiping the table, clearing away crumbs, and we were still eating. It was making me feel really awkward. Wherever I went, her mother went too. I was going to wash my underwear, and the moment I picked up the powder, she came into the bathroom and said:

"Oh, that's very expensive powder, I only use it in emergencies. You have to be very sparing, or there'll be none left soon."

I was flustered:

"I'm sorry, I didn't know."

She took a glass full of some powder out of a locker and said:

"Here, wash with this."

"Thank you."

She closed the door, and I was so nervous I dropped that glass and it broke. All day long Lena's mother walked around, saying:

"Our only glass tumbler is broken, the only one I could measure the washing powder with. Where am I going to get another glass like it now? It was very convenient, all my other ones are too big."

No matter what room I went into, she came in after me. I started getting so nervous that when I was drinking water or tea, I used to drop the cup, if I was eating, the fork used to drop out of my hand, or I was so agitated I jerked my plate and spilled the soup, because she was always fussing around beside me. She wouldn't let me eat or walk around or sleep in peace. Lena noticed this too, and she said to her mother:

"Mom, you've pissed me off with your cleanliness and neatness. Leave her in peace. Let her feel at ease, or I'll go back where I came from!"

Her mother was offended:

"I'm trying to oblige you, I just want everything in the house to be nice."

Lena answered:

"There's no need to oblige us, leave us alone. I came here to rest and celebrate the New Year with you! I'm tired of all these dishes and this cleaning, I'm fed up! But you're always fussing around with your plates and glasses and your cleaning, you take a break too, stop it."

Her mother burst into tears and went to her room.

In the morning I was getting washed in the bathroom. I washed my hair with some shampoo or other. Her mother came in again:

"Oh, oh, you used my expensive shampoo, you shouldn't have done that, ooh, ooh!" and she got out another shampoo for me, but I'd already finished washing my hair. I said:

"No thank you, I don't need it."

She got angry and went away.

Even when I was sitting in the toilet, she knocked and said: "Use the air freshener afterward, it's up on the top shelf, all right?"

I sat there thinking: She won't even—pardon the expression —let me shit in peace. I have to get out of here as quickly as I can.

During the days when we were at Lena's place, her father drove us round the collective farm settlements in his work car so that we could sell the rest of our goods. I sold almost all the goods, for Lena and for myself, because she said straightaway:

"I'm too shy to sell things. It turns out I'm no good at it. I'd better go back to Turkmenia."

And I answered her:

"It's all right for you, your parents are here, in Russia, and your child's with them" (her boy was in the seventh grade at school). "When you decide to move here, they'll do everything for you. You don't have to worry, your child is in safe hands: his grandfather and grandmother do the best they can for him, I can see that. But what have I got? My parents are in Uzbekistan. They live in a village, there's nothing there for children. I live in Turkmenia. My children don't know Uzbek and they don't understand Turkmenian either. But my mother-in-law wants to move to Russia, she says: 'My husband's dead, there's no one left here for me now, apart from my old mother. As soon as I bury her, I'll go away to Russia, to my homeland.' Lena, I have to arrange my own life, mine and my children's, for myself. You can see what's happening all around us. My boys go to the Russian school, when they graduate from school where will they go—to a college? Everything there's taught in Turkmenian. They might officially let them take the exams, but then they'll fail them, because they've got enough of their own kind. Let's suppose they have a sudden stroke of luck and they get into some higher educational institution. But when they graduate from college or technical college, who's going to give them a job? No one. Because everywhere the official records are kept in Turkmenian and everyone has to know the Turkmen language. But my boys don't know Turkmenian or Latin or Uzbek—in short, not a single word. So you can go back home, Lena, because everything will be arranged for you. I have to get everything for my children myself. Because I haven't got parents like you have—mine are simple and poor. They have enough cares in their life without me."

Lena and I celebrated the New Year 2000 with her parents. After that I said good-bye to them and left to go to Moscow. A day later I was sitting on the Kazan railroad station in Moscow, wondering which direction I should travel now. I looked at the train timetable: if I went to where my mother-in-law's nephew was, I'd be there in three or four hours. I walked over to the Leningrad Station and looked at the timetable: almost all the daytime trains arrived in Leningrad (that is, in Saint Petersburg) late in the evening. That wasn't good for me.

Because if I didn't find my friend or she'd changed her address, where would I go in the middle of the night? I thought I'd better go to the town that was four hours' journey from Moscow, where my mother-in-law's nephew Ravil lived with his wife Galya. I had the address, and I'd arrive there during the day, so I might find them quickly.

I bought a ticket for the train, for a private car, as there weren't any tickets left for the general one. For this pleasure I had to pay three times as much. I got out of the train at the right station and walked to where the taxis were standing, because I didn't know how to get where I was going on a trolley or a route taxi. I told the taxi driver the address and he said: "Let's go."

He asked me where I was from, who I had there and so on, the way all taxi drivers do, he was interested. When I told him the address, he said:

"If your relatives live at that address, it means they're well off."

I asked:

"Why do you think that?"

"It's a cooperative building, a big new one. People who buy apartments there have money."

I didn't answer him, because I'd never been to their place, how could I know how well off they were? Although my mother-in-law had told me her nephew used to work as a gold prospector.

The taxi driver dropped me off in front of a beautiful house, like the ones that belonged to the Soviet elite. I found the right entrance, and the floor and the apartment.

They were really happy to see me, as if it was the first time. They'd been at our house in Turkmenia, it's true, but that was a long time ago. Ravil's wife, Galya, said:

"Bibish, we want to tell you that tomorrow we're all going to Voronezh."

I asked:

"But why?"

"The thing is that Katya, my eldest daughter, is marrying a young man from Voronezh. They're going to have the wedding at the groom's house. If you like, you can come with us."

"No thank you," I said.

I had no smart clothes to wear for a wedding. And Galya wore size 60–62, two Bibishes would have fit in her clothes.

Early in the morning they went away. I stayed in their three-room apartment. It was true, everything there really was great: the layout of the rooms, and the European-style renovation.

I stayed there on my own, watching the television all day long—cable television, which we didn't have. It was interesting. But at night I was afraid of my own shadow. In a strange town, in a strange apartment . . . I was afraid to go even as far as the toilet and I waited until the morning. I ate everything there was in the refrigerator, I only went to the shop for bread, milk, and kefir.

A week later they came back from Voronezh with their son-in-law. It turned out that he'd moved in with them. Of course, I congratulated them and wished them all the best.

Now Ravil and Galya started asking me how it was I happened to be in Russia. I explained to them that I wanted my children to study, get married, and live in Russia, and I'd come in advance to reconnoiter. I was looking for a place where we could stay.

And then Galya started saying:

"Oh, life is bad in Russia now, everything's expensive, there's no work, the pay's low, it's impossible to live," and so on.

Ravil joined in too:

"Well, you've got here—and now what? You ought to have come sooner. If you'd come ten years ago, you'd have found a job and bought an apartment already. But what can you buy now? In some parts the apartments are too cheap, there's no point in selling. For that money you won't buy anything here in Russia. And renting an apartment is very expensive, and anyway no one's likely to take newcomers with children."

In short, they tried to dissuade me, as if I'd come to stay with them forever and was never going to go away. But I didn't give way to their arguments, I said:

"Even so, I'm going to try to stay here, especially since Moscow is so close."

Ravil asked:

"And what kind of work are you going to do?"

"I'll become a trader."

"Oh," said Galya, "for trading you need a license, and you have to have a place at the market, and they ask for your medical record too. And you have to have all the immunizations that we had when we were children . . ." and so on.

Both of them went on without stopping, and I really did wonder if it was all so unrealistic.

In the morning I got up early. They decided to help me. Galya went off to the market to talk to the manager there, she found me an empty stand and paid the woman who owned the stand for the place.

Then we went to Moscow together. We rode to the market in Cherkizovo in a private commercial bus, we had tickets there and back. Galya showed me everything I needed and I bought it all. We got back home safely. In the morning I went to the market and started trading without any papers and without a license.

In the meantime Ravil registered me in his apartment. After the market I brought home black bread, white bread, long loaves, kefir, milk, and eggs. But that wasn't enough for the day, because they had a lot of people at home: Ravil, Galya,

Katya, her husband, the second daughter, and me. We were all grown-ups, we ate a lot. So no sooner did I bring the bread home than it was gone.

I should say that Ravil and Galya were always arguing. Sometimes the arguments went on until the morning. I thought it was because of me. I was upset and so I said to Ravil:

"I'd like to leave the apartment, will you help me find an apartment?"

He started getting nervous and said, "No, let the newly-weds leave, I'm not keeping them here. They can look for an apartment for themselves. I told that little fool a hundred times: Katya, don't be in a rush, Katya, make a career, study, work. You can always get married. She didn't listen to me, she found herself some moron from a collective farm, and now they're both going to hang round my neck!"

"But why don't they go to Voronezh? You said yourself that he lives in Voronezh."

"Voronezh is no good! It's his father who lives in Voronezh, a miserable lush. He and his wife are divorced. And his son lived in the country with his grandmother, because they couldn't feed him. An aunt took one child and this one—my so-called son-in-law—stayed in the village. I arranged the wedding for them, on my own money. I bought a wedding dress for two thousand roubles and spent a whole lot of money beside that. Well, she put that dress on. We went to their village registry office. The door there was broken. I thought maybe we had to go to some other place. No, that ruin really was the registry office. We went back to the house and saw five or six old grandmothers with only one ninety-year-old granddad between them, sitting round the table, and that was all. There weren't any young people at all. I wondered why I'd spent my money, why I'd gone and bought a wedding dress for two thousand roubles, if the registry office had no doors and no one was at the table except old women and a ninety-year-old man. Katya's a lawyer by education, she went to college. Now because of this no-account jerk, she's thrown it all away—how do you like that!"

I thought this story was so funny, I could hardly stop myself laughing. Although, on the other hand, there was nothing funny about it, it was actually a very sad story.

But even so I asked Ravil to find me an apartment again.

That evening I wrote out several copies of an announcement: "Single woman seeks apartment. Phone . . ."

Ravil and I stuck this announcement up on lampposts, on a special board for announcements, on the bus and trolley stops, everywhere.

Then we started waiting for a call. Two days later a woman called and offered to let me live with her. Galya spoke to her and said we'd go take a look that evening.

And so we went to look at the apartment. The house turned out to be very close, just one stop away. The door was opened by an elderly woman, she was the one who'd called us. Galya settled all the arrangements and showed me to her. She agreed. We went for my things and came straight back. My landlady was called Nina Sergeevna, or just Aunty Nina.

But when I was living with them, Galya borrowed money from me—six hundred roubles—she said she'd give it back.

I began living with Aunty Nina, I got to know the neighbors: Aunty Lida, Aunty Masha, and lots of others.

After the market, in the evening, everybody used to gather at Aunty Nina's and play lotto, and they taught me how to play too. It was fun. Only things went very badly at the market, because it was January, one holiday after another—trade wasn't moving.

I phoned Turkmenia from Aunty Nina's place, reassured my husband, and said everything was all right with me. My mother-in-law took the phone and said:

"If it's very hard for you, come back, don't torment yourself." But until I'd found out about residence permits, registration, work, trade, school, college studies, and all the other things we would come up against in our life, I didn't want to go back. I walked all round the town and tried to find out about everything. Eventually, when things were more or less clear, I decided to go home and bought a ticket for the train. I agreed with Aunty Nina that if I came back with my children and husband, she would take us in.

* * *

Before I left, I phoned Galya and asked her to bring me the money, the six hundred roubles she had borrowed from me. There were two hours left until the train, it was time for me to leave, and she still hadn't come. Aunty Nina and her neighbor Aunty Lida decided to see me all the way to Moscow. Then Galya arrived and as she paid back her debt, she said rudely:

"There, take it! I've been all round the yard collecting that money!"

I thought it wasn't my fault, it was my money, wasn't it? I'd helped her and I'd suffered for it. But I didn't say anything out loud, I said good-bye to her and went to Moscow with Aunty Nina and Aunty Lida. They saw me to the Kazan Station and put me on the train. I promised to phone them and rode away, and then this is what happened to them, the poor things.

They took some money with them to buy a few things in Moscow. They saw me off and as they were walking away from the station, a crowd of gypsy women came toward them. The gypsies surrounded them and tricked them out of two thousand roubles each! My poor aunties, they lost so much money because of me, and they were pensioners!

I went home, taking presents to my children. It was horrible the way the soldiers at the station in Tashauz and on the border checked me! I couldn't even get home in peace. And they were insolent too, they spoke rudely to me. That kind of treatment immediately spoiled my mood. But I comforted myself: Be patient, Bibish, there's not much longer left. You'll never come back here again.

At home they were happy to see me. The children had missed me especially.

My husband and I spoke until late, discussing out future life. In short, we decided to move to Russia in the summer. We'd just received the papers for immigrant status. Now we could go without worrying. We sold off everything we had at home. There was nothing left. We didn't send off a container because the duty was very expensive, and we had no place of our own to put the things in.

I collected my children's documents from the school. We bought tickets for the train to Moscow. We said good-bye to the people we knew, our friends and relatives. I went to Uzbekistan to say good-bye to my parents. I said I wasn't likely to come back for the next five years, because the journey was very expensive, the trains weren't running, there was only a plane to Ashkhabad, and flying there and back cost about fifteen thousand roubles.

I bought a lot of melons and walnuts to treat Aunty Nina and her friends, and bought Iranian socks as a present for them. On the way, it's true, five of the melons went bad, they turned to liquid in the heat, and we threw them away. We didn't feel bad, we'd eaten lots of them during the summer.

* * *

Finally all our family arrived at Aunty Nina's place. She and the neighbor welcomed us warmly. Now every day in the morning my husband and I got up and went looking for work. But nobody took us on, because we hadn't deregistered from Turkmenia and we didn't have a permanent residence permit. We walked round the whole town. Where a job could be had, the pay was low, not even enough to pay the rent for the apartment. That was the situation we and the children were left in.

We had no money for a place of our own. For all the things we sold when we were leaving, we'd raised a thousand dollars. Even with that money it was impossible to buy anything —I mean a place to live.

They wouldn't give us a job without being registered. We began trying to persuade Aunty Nina to register us in her apartment, so that we could find work somewhere. But she had never had to deal with things like that before, and so she was afraid that if we were registered with her, we'd try to claim her flat. Of course, old people are afraid of everything. We had to explain for a long time that the registration was only a piece of paper, it would be valid for a certain time and there was no threat to her. But she wouldn't listen. Ten days went by. We still didn't have any work. It was a good thing Aunty Lida took our side:

"You lured the girl here, you said come, and I'll take you in, and now you're being difficult, surely you can see they're not getting anywhere. Registration's nothing to be afraid of. Register them, it won't kill you, and don't think they'll try to claim your apartment. If you don't believe me, go to a lawyer and ask, he'll give you the same answer. And don't put it off, go to the passport office with them."

Then Aunty Nina went to the passport office with us and registered us for six months.

Early in the morning I went to the local authority offices, waited my turn in line, and went into the office where they gave out licenses for trading. The woman sitting in the office said:

"We don't give licenses on a temporary registration."

I showed her the certificate saying I was a Russian citizen, but a newcomer, I had dual citizenship. She said:

"Your registration's only for six months, if it was for a year, I'd have given you a license."

I went back home and we begged Aunty Nina to register us again, this time for a year, because they hadn't given us a license. She didn't want to hear any more about it:

"No more, I've registered you for six months, and I'm not going round any more militia stations, I've got things of my own to do, the market garden. I told my son on the phone that I'd registered you, and he was so angry with me he hung up."

We could see that all our efforts were pointless. But we had to do something, not just sit there with our arms folded. In the morning I went off to a little town nearby and went into their municipal offices. I found out that they did give out licenses on a temporary registration, but in the regional center they didn't! I came back home and started thinking—maybe they did things differently in other regions? Before the children started school, maybe I could go to a different region and try to get registered, get a license, and find a job?

I left the children to my husband and set off on the bus to the town of Murom. In Murom I got in a train to Mukhtolov—that's already in the Gorki region—and then I ended up in the Kulebak district. Just see how far my idea took me! I walked round the buildings in the district, looking for a place to register, and in the end I didn't find anything. Lots of people wanted to let me live in their apartments, but no one wanted to register me there. I arrived back at the bus station tired and hungry. It was already late. The station was deserted. I went up to the ticket office and asked:

"Aren't there any buses?"

The woman in the ticket office answered:

"Where do you think you are, haven't you ever taken a bus before? The buses here follow the timetable, there aren't any more runs today. I'm afraid you're too late, sweetheart!"

"And what can I do now?" I started feeling nervous, it would soon be night.

"There'll be a bus in a minute, but it's going to the garage, that is to the bus park. I'll tell the driver to take you as far as the central highway. Wait there, all right? You can stop a car going your way."

The driver dropped me off on the highway and turned in the opposite direction. I stood in the road and kept holding my hand up all the time, but nobody stopped. There was forest all around. A little further along the road I saw a gas station. Almost all the vehicles were turning in there to fill up and then turning back. It was already dark and cold, and all I had on was a thin dress—when I set out from home I hadn't counted on being left on a highway at night in the middle of a forest.

Most of the vehicles driving past were trucks. They had space in their cabs, but I didn't try to stop them, because the drivers traveled with partners, and I was afraid. I stopped a few when I thought the driver was traveling alone: but when I opened the door of the cab, there was his partner sleeping. And the cars didn't stop.

Then it got completely dark. I was tired of standing and I was very afraid. I walked down off the road into the forest and dozed for a while under a birch tree. In the morning it started to rain and I was all wet, frozen, afraid, but I sat under the birch tree with my eyes closed the whole time so as not to feel my fear. Early in the morning I went back to the bus park and straightaway took the first bus to the railroad station. I reached Murom, then went home on a bus.

In short, my trip was a painful failure, I simply threw the money away.

*   *   *

I came back home on the same day they were showing the sinking of the atomic submarine *Kursk* on the television. The children and I were all upset, we hoped at least one of them would survive! But alas, it ended very sadly, and I felt terribly sorry for them. I couldn't get to sleep for a long time, I was tormented by insomnia and I was very upset.

Autumn was getting close. The children had to go to school.

I went to the nearest school, one that Aunty Nina had shown me—her children had gone there once as well. When I handed in the documents, they took them and said:

"Your children have been accepted for the school, but they have to be tested, and then we'll decide what grade they'll go into."

The first of September came, my children's long-awaited first day at school—their first in Russia. They were tested. My older son, Aibek, was accepted into a class where the students were weak, or had some kind of disability, or had no mother or father.

I asked:

"Why put him there?"

They told me:

"He was slow in solving the problems and the math questions during the testing."

But my second son, Nadirbek, was accepted into a very good class. Aunty Nina brought some beautiful flowers from her dacha. Then we dressed the children up smartly and sent them to school with flowers for the teachers. I went with them, they were really happy.

My husband and I decided to go to the migration center. We had the document about our immigrant status. We went into the office where they processed newcomers from the former USSR.

In the office a thin man with a mustache looked at us in surprise and said:

"But why did you come here anyway?"

I answered:

"For the sake of the children."

"We can't do anything to help you, you have Russian citizenship, you have to do everything for yourselves."

I said to him:

"We don't have a permanent residence permit."

"I don't know, I don't know, go to some rural district and arrange life for yourself there. By the way, you came from Turkmenia, but if you'd come from Uzbekistan, we could have helped you."

"Why's that, what difference does it make where we came from? The fact is that we're Russian citizens too, here are our documents."

He stuck to his line:

"Your president and Putin have an agreement," and he

began to explain. But in the end I still didn't understand a thing, and we went back to the apartment.

You see, a state is an abstraction, but the people living in it are real individuals. Different concepts. It can be hard for the two to reach an agreement.

Two weeks went by.

After their main school the children went to the music school—piano, grade two. Both of them could already play four pieces. I always went with them, we used to ride to the music school on a trolley, and I waited for them there, because they didn't know the town very well yet, even I didn't. I had heaps of time to fuss over them, as you can understand, I didn't have any work to do.

The children were doing well at the main school and at the music school. I thought everything was going well, although a few times Aibek—he was ten—complained that they called him names at school—"black face," "black ass," "black sheep," "tramp," "beggar," "nigger" (he's not anything like a black man, although he has a dark complexion)—and hit him hard in the head.

One day he came home all beaten up.

"Mom, dye my hair brown so I won't be different from all the others, so that they won't notice me. Mom, do something.

Why did you have me so dark, couldn't you have had me light-colored?"

And my second son, Nadirbek, told me:

"Mom, everyone in school talks about how they gave my brother"—and he pointed at Aibek—"a real good beating. I'm sick of it all. The kids laugh because my brother's weak and he can't defend himself."

My husband and I scolded our children:

"Be quiet, it's not all that simple. They'll soon get used to you. It's not so terrible. Be patient. We've got loads of problems as it is, you can see, we can't find any work at all! And if they call you names or hit you, you complain to the teachers!"

The children told us:

"We did complain to the teachers, they listened to our complaints, then they gave the boys a telling off, but it was useless, they still beat us up."

"Then when they beat you, try to lie on the floor and don't get up until the teacher comes. Maybe then the boys will start to feel a little bit sorry for you!" Those were the terrible words I said to them.

And again they told us:

"We tried that, we fell on the ground and didn't get up, but they just kicked Aibek, he can never fight back."

Sometimes three or four boys, sometimes just two, one day from one class, the next day from another, would attack my older son. Every day there were insults, name-callings, or beatings. When he complained, I told him, like a fool:

"Listen, I'm not going to go looking round the classrooms every day to find the boys who beat you. It's impossible to find them, just you be patient, some time it will all stop."

And then our patience was rewarded.

The Story of What Happened to Aibek

I thought there could be nothing more terrible than what had happened to me in my childhood. I was wrong. This time the victim was my little ten-year-old son.

It happened on September 14.

My children came home from school. I fed them and we set off to the music school. All the way Aibek walked very slowly, and I scolded him:

"Can't you walk any faster, we're late for the class."

He answered in a faint voice:

"Mom, my legs are tired, my head's spinning, and it hurts real bad."

But I didn't look at him, I only scolded him:

"You're pretending, you just don't want to do your class, come on, get a move on!"

Then Nadirbek couldn't stand it anymore:

"Mom, are you blind or something? They strangled him in school today, take a good look at his neck—they almost killed him."

I stopped and looked and saw the bluish-pink marks of fingers on my son's neck! I froze. I felt as awful as if he was already dead. We were standing in the road, and I was thinking feverishly about what I should do.

It was the end of the working day, about four o'clock. But we went back to their school and just happened to meet Aibek's grade teacher. I couldn't help myself, my tears were flowing down. I explained everything to her as well as I could. She looked at his neck straightaway and kept saying:

"How terrible! How terrible!"

Then she took us to the home of that boy, the "sadistic monster." His grandmother, grandfather, and sister were there.

It turned out that the boy's mother had been deprived of her parental rights and his father was in prison. Yes, the boy admitted to us that he really had strangled Aibek. I began sobbing and I said to that boy:

"If you hate him, if you really don't like him, call him any names you like, even 'black ass,' even 'nigger,' only don't kill my son." And I screamed and cried.

Now that everything was clear, I felt sorry for the old people: there was no way they could control this child, he already had a police record although he was only ten.

After the painful explanation we went back home and Aibek said:

"Mom, my hands are shaking and my head hurts real bad."

I put him to bed. He didn't sleep properly, he raved and coughed terribly and tossed about all night long and cried out in his sleep.

In the morning I looked at his neck again. I could clearly see the marks of little fingers on it. We had breakfast and my older son didn't go to school, but my second one did.

I stayed with Aibek. I began asking him how it had happened.

It turned out that what had happened was this:

Five boys from his class had called him into the English classroom and started taunting him. They said:

"Let's fight!"

Aibek answered:

"There's one of me and five of you, I'm not going to fight you," and he tried to walk away.

Then the "boy hero" shouted:

"Coward!" and he wouldn't let him go, he hit him and started strangling him. The other pupils stood there and watched as if it was some kind of exciting game, and they helped the "hero" and kicked Aibek. One boy even counted:

"One . . . two . . . three . . . four . . . five . . ." like in a boxing ring. They were curious to see how long Aibek could hold out without any air.

My son went on with his story:

"When I tried to shout 'Help, save me!' I didn't have any voice and nobody heard me."

Everything went black, and his head started to spin, but the "hero" went completely wild and squeezed even harder. My son had already lost consciousness and fallen on the floor, but the "boy hero" strangled him again and shouted:

"Die, black ass! I won't let you go until I kill you."

At that moment by chance, completely by chance, some senior students opened the door of the classroom . . . It was only then that the boy let Aibek go, and by a miracle he was still alive. If there hadn't been any more lessons in that English classroom and the senior students hadn't come in, my son wouldn't be alive now, he would have been dead long ago.

"Mom," he said, "I didn't have any air at all. Now I understand how bad the sailors felt on the *Kursk* submarine without any air."

I put my son to bed and covered him so that he could have a rest. I went out into the kitchen. My husband attacked me there:

"I don't want a dead child! We don't even have anywhere to bury a dead child! We'd have to put him in a hole somewhere, like a dead dog! I didn't come here so that my children could be killed for nothing! Go where you like, but I won't let the child go to school. What guarantee is there, tell me, that everything will be all right with him from now on? They've only been at school for fourteen days! Just think! . . . And all that time they've called him names and beaten him almost every day. How much can he put up with? You're the one to blame! What did we come here for? To cripple our children, was that it?"

He shouted so terribly, but you can understand the state he was in!

What could I do then?

I phoned the police. They told us to come in, and I went to them with my son. We went into an office. There was a young inspector sitting there. He asked:

"What happened?"

"Yesterday in school my son was strangled."

"What's that? Where is he?"

"Here he is, sitting bedside me. I want you to do something about it."

The officer said, "So he's not dead, then?"

An answer like that made my jaw drop and I asked myself: Does that mean he had to die for the police to do anything? Very funny. Then what did I come here for? It turns out the police won't do anything unless someone dies!

"Write a complaint!" said the policeman. "Write how it all happened, and go to the forensic medical expert."

We went for a forensic medical examination. There were a lot of people there. Alcoholics standing there with black eyes and some students who were beaten up, too.

Finally our turn came. We went into the office where they did the examinations.

An elderly woman doctor met us. She checked everything very carefully and began scolding me:

"Why didn't you come sooner, strangulation means death, your son didn't have much chance left. You say yourself they were calling him names and beating him. Why did you put up with it for so long? You ought to have done something about it straightaway, the school has a director after all, there's a class teacher. If things go on like this, you won't have a child! And you," she said to my son, "need to play sports, you must defend yourself, sports will help you, do you understand?"

I said to her:

"I have two of them, they both do music lessons, they play the piano, they're already in the second grade."

The doctor dismissed that out of hand:

"Music and the piano will always be there. Just at the moment the children need to play sports. Sports will always be useful to them in life. Here's a forensic medical examination certificate for you. All the best to you, look after the children!"

After that happened, the district education committee came to the school, held a parents' meeting and a teachers' meeting, and the local police came. Some meetings were about my son.

Soon the director of the school sent for me and began saying to me:

"It's the first time this has happened in our school, there's never been anything like it before. I've already moved your son into the very best class. If he doesn't like it there, we'll move him to a different class, only please, take back your complaint to the police. You can see we've taken measures, called in the parents and the teachers, held a meeting about your son. Of course, I sympathize with you, but at least he's still alive. Please, take back your complaint."

I couldn't hold myself back at that:

"Listen, you think that I'm a newcomer, that I don't know the language, I don't know the laws, but there's one thing I'm a hundred percent sure of—if instead of me it was some Chechen woman and her son who'd been treated the way my son has, not only would she kill the boy who did it, she'd put a bomb under the entire school. I'm absolutely sure of that, their revenge is very cruel, and they have no pity for anyone."

The director said:

"Yes, yes, of course. But you know, I'm a migrant too. We're from the Far East. My husband was a military man, he retired. So ten years ago we came here. I heard that you're renting an apartment, I know all about that. My husband and I lived in various apartments for a long time before we were given our own. I worked in the summer, I wanted to go on leave in September. Because of this business my superiors won't give me any leave, and my sick mother's back there . . . Perhaps you will take back your complaint?"

I felt sorry for her and I agreed. I went to the precinct and I took back my complaint.

But meanwhile, it turned out that the local officer had been to the apartment, and the class supervisor had come as well.

Aunty Nina couldn't stand any more. I could see her patience was exhausted.

"I have enough problems of my own," she said. "I don't need any more headaches. Please don't be offended, but find yourself another apartment."

Well how do you like that, that was all we needed! No job, our child had almost been killed, and now we were going to be out in the street.

I went to Aunty Lida straightaway:

"Help me find another apartment, please."

Aunty Lida was surprised:

"What's bitten Nina? All right, what difference does it make now? We'll have to look for an apartment."

I didn't just sit around with my arms folded either, I started going round the agencies and calling the numbers in the announcements, but it was the same answer everywhere:

"They don't take non-Russians, the landladies won't agree to it. And especially with children."

Poor Aunty Lida walked round the houses until ten o'clock in the evening, looking for an apartment for us. It was hard, but she found one. She phoned in the evening:

"I've got a friend here, he's living on his own just now, his son's staying with some woman. I persuaded him, and he's agreed. You know yourself, a bit of extra money never hurts. I'll take you there tomorrow, and you can settle up with Nina later, when she comes back from her dacha, and you can move to the new apartment, all right? By the way, your landlord won't be there for a long time, he's going into the hospital tomorrow for an operation. While he's there, you'll be on your own. Listen, I wanted to ask you something, Bibish. You said you were in the municipal offices, didn't you? And they didn't give you a license there, and since then you've been sitting at home and doing nothing? You shouldn't be sitting at home, you've got children, a family. You know it yourself, money runs away like water—if you don't work, your reserves are soon gone. Always remember: if they refuse you in one office or they won't listen to you, you go and knock on another door!"

I laughed and said to her:

"As soon as we move to the other apartment, I'll go round knocking at office doors, all right."

Aunty Lida helped me a lot: She looked after my children, took them to the forest and to swim and showed them the town. While we were looking for work, she took the children to her place and fed them, because Aunty Nina was at the dacha all the time. We even went to help her harvest the potatoes. That year she had a good harvest. She was very fond of her vegetable garden. At the town show she exhibited her own sorts of tomatoes, potatoes, onions, and pumpkins, and she won first place.

In the autumn I settled up with Aunty Nina and we said good-bye. I was grateful to her; after all, she did register us for six months.

At our new place we got on with the landlord immediately. He showed us everything, told us what we could do and what we couldn't, and said:

"Tomorrow morning I'm going into the hospital. I'll come out fit and well, God willing, and we'll get to know each other a bit better. Here's the key, make yourselves at home, good night!"

He was called Alexander Ivanovich, or Uncle Sasha. Before he went to bed he came out of his room again:

"Another thing I wanted to tell you: You should move the children to our school, it's very close, only a couple of steps away, we can even hear the bell. Otherwise you'll have to wait for the trolley in winter, and anything could happen on the way. Here you don't have to take a briefcase anywhere, or a change of shoes. Oh, all the things your children have to carry around, and they're still so little. Think about it, think about what I told you, all right?"

He had a urological illness: his urine dripped out through a tube into a bottle. That was why he was going into the hospital, so that they could operate and remove the tube.

And another thing he said was:

"I won't lock my room. If you like, I have an accordion in there, the children can practice on it. If you like to read, there are books. So go in, I haven't got any money lying around, I don't need to lock anybody out of the room."

In the morning he left for the hospital. We got up. I tidied up everywhere and aired the apartment because it smelled of urine. I bought an air freshener and sprayed everywhere. And I went into his room, intending to change his bed. When I looked the sheet and the quilt cover were saturated with urine. Probably when Uncle Sasha was lying down, urine ran onto the bed from the tube. I stripped the bed, put the mattress on the balcony, and soaked the bedsheets, then washed them and ironed them. My husband dealt with the bathroom and the toilet, cleaned them and disinfected them. We tidied and cleaned everywhere, put everything in order. And we swept the stairs down to the entrance with a twig broom.

By the way, when I was living with Aunty Nina, I always swept the entrance for everyone and wiped down the stairs. Because all the people there were old, and I felt sorry for them. We got on well, we were friends. We used to visit each other almost every day.

But there were all sorts of people living on that staircase too. One elderly woman spent her free time walking round the streets collecting empty bottles. Then she handed them in. And that woman didn't acknowledge anyone who wasn't Russian. When she saw me, she always used to ask:

"Do you know what day it is today?"

"No, I don't."

"Today's a big holiday. Don't do the washing, don't sweep the floor."

"Why?"

"That's the custom here. If you live in Russia, you have to observe our customs."

"Well, I respect all customs, but when I have a holiday, I don't try to tell other people what to do or what not to do."

"And I tell you: since you live here, you have to obey our traditions."

"And if I go to Mongolia I have to live like the Buddhists, and in Italy like the Catholics, is that it? I have my own faith, here inside me, and I don't force it on anyone. And I advise you not to try to force yours on me!"

She was very offended, she walked off, and for a long time after that she grumbled and complained to the neighbors that what I said was wrong and what I did was wrong.

Several times I went out early in the morning with a big plastic sack and collected empty bottles on the sidewalks and in the park. Mostly I found beer bottles. They smelled so terrible!

I wasn't embarrassed at all. I collected a full plastic sack every time and brought it to that woman so that she wouldn't be angry and try to tell me what customs to observe.

In principle she was a good person. She was just obsessed with the question of Russian and non-Russian. So I'm not Russian—what am I supposed to do, die? The way God made me, that's what I am. People all love their own nation. I love mine too, but I'm not going to make others suffer because of it. If you think like that woman, there'll be quarrels and resentment, there'll be evil, and in the end there'll be war.

But you can't convince an old person. It's better to put up with it.

* * *

A day went by. Early in the morning I set out for the school that Uncle Sasha had recommended to us. Yes, the school really was close to our house, and we could even hear the bell from the apartment.

In the school I was seen by the head teacher, and I told her about what had happened to my son. She said:

"All right, bring the documents, and bring the children at the same time. I'll get to know them and assign them to classes."

I ran to the old school for the documents, collected them, and went to the head teacher with the children. She had a talk with them and she was astonished:

"We always expect backward children from Central Asia, recently some new pupils came to us—they speak really poor Russian. We're having real trouble with them. But your children even speak without any accent, they answered my questions very well. Where did they learn to do that?"

"My mother-in-law," I answered, "is half Russian, and my husband graduated from the Russian school. Since they were little my mother-in-law looked after them, she sang them lullabies, read them Russian fairytales. Then my children were in the Russian group at kindergarten, and after that we put them in the Russian school, and the result is that they don't know their own language, and they don't want to know it, and they even scold me: 'Don't babble in Chukcha to us, mom,' they say. It's because of them that we came here."

"Very good. Let's go to classroom 5A, and I'll introduce Aibek to the children, and we'll take your second son to the office of the head teacher of elementary classes."

We went into classroom 5A. The pupils stood up, the head teacher said hello to them and began explaining:

"Boys and girls, a new pupil has come to join you, he's called Aibek, and not long ago something tragic happened to him. I'm warning you: no name-calling, no beatings. I hope you understand me, all right?"

And now, knock on wood, they've been going to that school for more than two years without anything terrible happening.

But then, after that business Aibek became absentminded. All the things that he put on for school—his cap, his jacket, his school shoes, his boots—one by one, he left them all at school, forgot them, and in the morning no one could find anything. He cried in his sleep for a long time as well. And during the day he felt weak and humiliated.

The children had to give up music. I put them in a sports club to do judo and sambo. My second son's already doing well at everything. Aibek, as always, is lagging behind.

Those are the kinds of problems my children have had here in Russia.

Just as Aunty Lida had told me, I went to the municipal offices again—to knock on all the doors: I went into the building and set off round the offices. I opened one door, and a lot of women were sitting at computers. They asked me:

"What do you want?"

But I couldn't explain properly. They sent me to a different office, to their boss. I went to the boss. I knocked on the door and opened it. I saw a woman sitting there. I said to her:

"If they don't understand me here, I'll probably die."

She received me kindly:

"What's the matter? Sit down, calm down, and tell me everything from the beginning. I'm listening to you."

I told her everything: that I had all the documents, that I was a Russian citizen, but I had no resident permit and only a six-month registration. Because of that they wouldn't give me a license, we just sat at home, the money we'd brought was running out, and so on . . . She said:

"You can't go and die, you have to feed your children. I saw an even worse case than yours: A woman brought some petrol, soaked herself from head to foot, and wanted to set fire to herself. She had children too, a Russian woman. When she moved here to Russia from somewhere else, they stole everything she had in the train—her money and her things, there was nothing left. We barely managed to calm her down, and we helped her settle in. After that everything was fine. So stop thinking about dying. Have you been to the migration center?"

"Yes."

"Now go there again and ask them if they're going to solicit your case. If they refuse, come back here immediately, and then I'll tell you what to do. Do you understand?"

"Yes!"

"Then go to the migration center and come back to me!"

I ran to the migration center and explained to them, they said:

"You have citizenship of the Russian Federation, you have nothing to do with us. Ask for everything you need from the municipal administration, we're not going to solicit for your application!" After that answer I went running back to the woman at the municipal center. She was expecting me.

"I knew it," she said. "I knew they'd refuse. All right, never mind. Then write an application to the chairman of the Soviet of deputies, I'll dictate it to you." And she dictated it.

She took me and the application and we walked round all the floors, she went into the office of the chairman of the Soviet of deputies, explained my situation and solicited for my application. (To be quite honest, to this day I don't know what the word "solicit" means, so there you are.) We went back to her office and she said:

"There, you see, it's all settled. Now I'll make a phone call, and tomorrow they'll give you a license to trade. And you wanted to die! How cunning you are—planning to abandon two children! It won't work! Now you can go, everything will be all right for you now."

"Thank you, I don't know how to thank you."

"No need to thank me, it's my job. When I can help some-one, I think it's been a good day!"

I said good-bye to her and almost burst into tears, I was so happy.

I went dashing to the wholesale shop, and bought some boxes of candy and coffee. I went back to the municipal build-ing and into her office. She saw me and was surprised:

"What else has happened now?"

"Nothing's happened, in our parts they say you can't put a thank-you in your pocket. Take these, please, they're for you."

She said:

"No, I won't take them. Give them to the children, let them eat them."

"Take them, they're for you, with all my heart!"

"No-no, you'd better give them to the children from me, say Aunty Tonya asked you to."

Probably I tried to persuade her for about twenty minutes, but she didn't take my gifts. And I went back to the apart-ment happy. After all, I wanted to pay my taxes honestly, not like some people who take off like rabbits. I just wanted every-thing to be official.

And that was how my commercial activity began. After two months the management of the market allocated us a defi-nite place, but before that we were hopping from one stall to another every day. In the end that was settled too. I went to Moscow every week for the goods—shoes and clothes.

Our landlord was in the hospital for exactly three months. I visited him often. Uncle Sasha had had his operation, and no longer had a tube now. And they'd taken away the bottle for urine.

"I was married twice, from the first marriage there are two children, and there are two children from the second marriage too. I used to be a boss, I had everything—money and friends. But now I've gotten old, I've retired, I'm sick . . . I'm ashamed to admit that apart from you no one has visited me in the hospital—not my friends, not my children. I still don't really know you, and we haven't lived together yet, and you've shown such concern for me. Thank you! As soon as I get out of hospital, we'll get to know each other better, all right?"

"Alexander Ivanovich, some day we'll get old too and we could find ourselves in the same situation, and so old people should be respected."

But he shook his head and said:

"In your parts, in the East, it's the custom to respect old age, but in Russia everything's different, they treat old people with less respect."

The children went to school and my husband and I traded, after all, we had a license now.

By the way, I met many interesting people at the market. People end up there in various ways, you know. Among the traders there are doctors, teachers, even former actors. Usually they don't like to talk about how they ended up there. Life works out differently for everyone. But everyone has to feed their children, that's the way it is.

At the market all sorts of funny things were always happening to me. And all because of my "knowledge" of Russian! That was why the trade wasn't going well—before I could find the right word, the customer would walk away.

The market traders often used different Russian words like *privozit'* (to bring), *zavozit'* (to drop off), *navozit'* (to bring in) to mean "deliver." And I wondered: Why do they use such long words and different forms? You can shorten the word. One time a woman came up to me and asked:

"How much is the denim shirt?"

"Two hundred and fifty roubles. Take it, it's very good, they only brought it recently. It's still a new delivery." Only I used the word *navoz* for "delivery," and that means "manure."

That was what I said: "It's still new manure."

Another customer came up to me and asked about a leather jacket.

"A good jacket," I said. "It costs a thousand five hundred roubles. Only one left from the old manure."

My husband heard me frightening away the customers, and he got angry:

"What's this you've been saying, for pete's sake! 'old manure,' 'new manure' . . . As if you were trading in shit. Next time, think what you're saying!"

One time an old woman came up to me and asked:

"Daughter, how much are your boots?"

"What kind do you want?"

"Well, so it's easy for me to put them on and take them off."

"Choose the kind you're looking for. Here, I've got these galoshes for you!"

"Yes, but are they comfortable?"

"Very comfortable and soft. Try them on, perhaps they'll fit you."

"I'm size forty. Daughter, find my size for me."

I found size 40 and she began trying the boots on. I asked the old woman:

"Well, how are they?"

"I haven't got them on yet."

I wanted to explain to the old woman that the boots were just the right size for her. So I used the Russian word that I thought meant "calf" or "boot top"—*vlagalishche*.

"You have a very big vagina," I said, "that's why I took out a big one especially, it ought to fit."

She didn't look at me, she bent down, tried to put on the boot.

I said it again:

"Everybody has narrow vaginas, but you've got a big one."

She didn't hear me or pretended not to.

"You have a lovely vagina, there aren't many vaginas like that. My customers usually have narrow vaginas, it's hard for them to choose boots. But you're lucky."

I talked about her vagina like that for about ten minutes. I praised it every possible way.

It was as if the poor old woman didn't hear me at all. She bought those boots and went away. Then I forgot about it.

But at home, at Uncle Sasha's place, there was a medical book. One day I decided to look through it in my free time. Suddenly I saw the word *vlagalishche*—and I almost fainted. Only then did I learn what it means! And I'd been using it instead of the word *golenishche*, which means boot top! It was a good thing the old woman wasn't listening to me very carefully, wasn't it!

And it was ages before I could learn that Russian word *golenishche*, for a long time I used to say either *golenilishche* or *goleninishche*.

Another time a young man and a girl came up to me and they asked me:

"Do you have Coffin?" They used the Russian word *grob*.

I was surprised:

"What do you want a coffin for, you're so young, you should live, you still have everything ahead of you."

"It's fashionable now."

"That's strange, how can there really be a fashion like that? You should get married, you should have children, what's all the hurry, you always have time to die!"

199

"Woman, I think you probably didn't understand, did you?"

"No, why, I did. What do you want a coffin for?"

"Woman, you didn't understand me. It's a designer brand, and you're lecturing me about life!"

"Ah, why didn't you say it was a brand? Imagine that, the fools thinking up a brand called 'Coffin.'"

In fact the shoes weren't called that at all. It wasn't *grob*, but "Gabor," I think.

So that was how the story of that "coffin" ended.

One time another customer came up to me:

"How much are your shirts?"

"A hundred fifty roubles."

"And do you have all sizes?"

"Yes, all sizes, choose."

"And if it doesn't fit, can I change it?"

"Yes, of course, I'll give away any size."

And she paid her money. I said to her:

"Come back if it's too small, I'll give away any size."

She was surprised:

"Woman, what do you mean by 'give away' if I pay money for it?"

"What did I say that was bad?"

"You're not giving it away to me at all, I'm buying it for my money."

"And what should I say?"

"Say 'I sell.'"

"Well, I'm sorry—it's not 'I give away,' but 'I sell.'"

"Now that's right."

One time I offended a trader at the market, a woman we knew. Her husband was in the army. Because of that everybody used to call her the "army woman." They didn't know her name. Then one day I asked her:

"Excuse me, please, what's your name, you know when we see you we say: 'The army woman's coming!'"

She laughed and answered:

"My name's Masha."

And I remembered that for the Russians the affectionate form for Nastya is Nastenka, for Galya it's Galochka, for Nina it's Ninochka. I wanted to use her affectionate name too, and so I said "Mashínka," but that's the Russian for a small automobile.

She took offense:

"Just what kind of car do you think I am?"

"I wanted it to be affectionate, did it turn out the opposite? What did I say wrong?"

"The stress is wrong, and that made it an automobile."

"And how should I say your affectionate name?"

"You should say 'Máshenka'! It's a good thing you don't know Russian, if you had said that knowing Russian, I'd soon show who's the car around here!"

Perhaps she thought I meant her figure? So you see, I made a real mess even with the stresses.

* * *

But once my language really did lead me a long astray. I needed to go to the toilet, and that's at the collective farm market, not the goods market. I was walking there and suddenly a young woman spoke to me:

"Woman, are you in a hurry?"

"No, what did you want?"

"Oh, I'm in a great hurry, could you show this old man to the bread store? He's blind and he walks very slowly. I have to run to work, I'm late already. Will you take him there?"

"Yes, of course!"

"Only hold on to him, or he'll fall!"

I took the old man by the arm, and then I remembered my husband. There was a phrase he liked to repeat: "Well, how did you come to such a life, my old chum?" I decided I could start a conversation with this old man with that phrase, and I said:

"Well, how did you come to such a life, old chum?"

He stopped, and even though he couldn't see me, because he was blind, he turned toward me, he was so astonished. And then he began answering that question of mine in detail. He told me how he was born and how he grew up, who he was, where he worked and about his children, and so on. And he walked along like a tortoise or even slower. I said to him:

"But where's your wife?"

"My wife was killed in a plane crash," and he started telling me about her. We walked very slowly, probably for about an hour, and we still hadn't reached the store. I still needed to go to the toilet. And I couldn't just abandon the old man in the street. I carried on with the conversation:

"When your wife died, you probably felt very bad, did you?"

He stopped again and said angrily:

"She didn't die, she was killed!"

I thought: What did I say that was bad? What's the difference between "was killed" and "died"? But it turned out that "she died" is when she did it herself and "she was killed" is when it was someone else's fault. That's the way it is.

I barely managed to get the old man to the bread shop and from there to the trolley stop. After two hours I came back to the market and my husband.

He was terribly nervous.

"What did you do, fall into the toilet? I've been waiting, you were gone for ages!"

I barely managed to calm him down so I could start trading.

Finally Alexander Ivanovich came out of the hospital and we began living together and getting on very well. He almost always corrected me if I spoke incorrectly, and he even got upset when I pronounced words badly.

The New Year 2001 arrived. Uncle Sasha went away to celebrate it with friends. Not long before he left we gave each other presents. And then we were on our own. At ten o'clock in the evening there was a ring at the door. We opened it and there were Ravil and his wife standing there. They'd come to celebrate the New Year with us. Well, all right. They sat and talked, and they drank (I don't drink, after all).

When I moved to that town with my family, Ravil's mother had given us five kilograms of dried apricots to pass on to him and she'd also warned us not to pester him with any questions about a place to live or about a job. She said:

"Don't bother my son."

We answered:

"All right, we get the hint. We'll live a long way away from them, so as not to bother them unnecessarily."

We'd only spoken to them on the phone once and told them that we'd brought those apricots. That time they'd invited us to visit them, and that was all, we hadn't seen them after that. Now they'd probably found us through Aunty Nina, and so they'd come to celebrate the New Year.

It turned out that the mother of their son-in-law had come to see them from Voronezh. Since they still weren't on good terms with their son-in-law, they didn't want to celebrate the holiday with him, so they'd left them and come to us. They stayed until three in the morning and then said good-bye.

On January 2 they came again, and even brought their neighbors—a husband and wife—with them.

That time Uncle Sasha was sitting in his room. Ravil asked:

"Well then, are you all right here?"

"Yes, everything's fine."

Galya said:

"Ravil and I thought and thought a lot and we've decided we're going to take you away from here."

"Where to?"

"To us, you're going to live beside us."

"No, we're fine here, the landlord's a good man, the children's school is close by, and nothing's happened to them there. The children are already used to the school, and so we won't move them anywhere else again."

"Everything you earn goes on the rent for the apartment. If things go on like that, you'll never be able to save up enough money for a place of your own."

"You have enough family of your own at home, there'd be too many of us, what would you want that for?"

Galya explained:

"But you're not going to live with us, only on our staircase. There's an empty apartment there, three rooms. Actually, the work on it needs to be finished. The woman it belongs to is a friend of mine, she lives in Urengoi, in the north. She hardly ever comes here. I've got the key. She always used to send the money for the apartment by mail, and I paid it here. I'll phone her, and if she says it's all right, you'll live right beside us, and you'll only have to pay for one person, because there's only one person registered there. You must agree, it's a very good option for you."

"But doesn't she work, then, won't she come herself?"

"No, she works an awful lot. Something terrible happened to her daughter. When her daughter was five, a drug addict stabbed her grandmother to death. The little girl was so frightened she ran out into the street, fell down on the snow, and then couldn't get up again. She's been paralyzed since she was five. Now she's sixteen, she's had eleven operations. Her operations are always done in Leningrad. Last year the woman who owns the apartment came and wanted to do European-style repairs, she ripped everything out of the apartment: she took up the linoleum, took away the bath, the sink, the toilet bowl. Then they phoned her from Urengoi to say her daughter was unwell, so she dropped everything and went away. Now we don't know when she'll come. If you have time, come tomorrow to take a look at the apartment. Think over our suggestion."

And they went home. My husband and I wondered what we ought to do. We felt all right at Uncle Sasha's place, there were no conflicts, only it was cramped—there were four of us in one room. One of my sons slept on a folding bed, because there was no room for a real bed.

In the morning we went to the building where Ravil and Galya lived. They opened the door into the empty apartment for us. There were three huge rooms, and you could simply get lost in the kitchen. We liked that it was so spacious, but there were repairs that needed to be done.

We said: "All right, we'll move in here. Only first the repairs have to be finished off." We bought everything that was needed and repaired the apartment.

We went to say good-bye to Uncle Sasha. He said:

"Well, what can I say, if you think it's better there, it's up to you. The most important thing is that you don't have any grudges against me. If you're not happy there, with your relatives—come back, I'll take you in. You can rely on me."

We began to live beside our relatives. When we were bored, we went to visit Uncle Sasha. We didn't move the children to a different school, why traumatize them like that?

Ravil went to Moscow almost all the time on business trips, but Galya never worked.

We'd only lived in the new apartment for about a week when we started to have problems. Galya kept borrowing money from us, and she didn't give it back for a long time. And we thought: Surely she must understand that we keep moving from one apartment to another with two children, we need money ourselves like the air we breathe. And they'd got along as man and wife for twenty years before we came. Had they really been waiting for us so they could borrow money?

We never refused Galya—however much money she asked for, we gave it to her, and Ravil didn't know about it. Then she started asking us to lend money to her girlfriends as well as to her. We didn't refuse them either, we gave it to them without saying anything. But then, her friends always paid the money back on time, not like Galya.

We always felt tense now, because Galya had begun creating scenes. One time she came and said:

"Turn the television down! The neighbors are complaining!"

And another time:

"Ravil came home and he scolded me: Go and talk to them, you're related, after all!"

She didn't know when to stop—she used to wake us up at six in the morning and in the middle of the night. She didn't care that she was disturbing our peace. She knocked on the door and shouted:

"Save me, Ravil's killing me!"

She played tricks like that quite often, and at the same time she never thought of paying back the money she owed us.

One time she came and asked me:

"If your husband swore at you or beat you all the time and drove you out of the house, what would you do?"

I said:

"We have enough problems without quarreling. If he swears at me, I keep quiet, because in a little while he calms down."

"How can you put up with it? That's the last thing you need. They put up with that in your parts, in the East, but this is Russia!"

"I can't get divorced just because of a few insults and make my children orphans. Children need a father. No one can take the place of their father."

In short, there was no way I could persuade her and calm her down. We agreed to differ. We lived in that house and were friends with the neighbors. It was only Galya who got on our nerves with her shouting and her tears and her quarrels with Ravil.

Nine months went by. In that time we were able to buy a color television on our savings. And that was all, nothing else.

The fall began. November. In the middle of the month Galya announced:

"Pack up your things, the owner of the flat's coming. She wants to sell it."

"When do we have to leave?" was all I asked.

"Tomorrow if you like. Look for a new place to live."

"Winter's coming on, while we're looking, before we find a place . . . Can we wait another week?"

"No, the owner is coming. She phoned and said: 'I want them to leave the flat urgently.'"

My husband and I were very upset. What could we do? We went to see Uncle Sasha, where we used to live. We explained the situation to him. He said:

"You really shouldn't have left me. It's always the same with relatives. It's best to live as far away from them as you can. And I've already got other lodgers."

"Oh no!"

"Oh yes! My friends found them for me, because I needed the money. They've been living with me for a few days already, a young couple with a little child, one year old. I can't throw them out in the street, it's winter already. How can they throw you out like that without any warning?"

"It just happened!"

"You have children too, they shouldn't have treated you like that. And where are you going to go now?"

"Where? Out into the street, to look for an apartment. Maybe we'll find one, maybe we won't—we don't know."

We said good-bye to Uncle Sasha and went back home. Every day Galya turned up like an earthquake. She shouted at us. It was impossible to put up with it any longer. Recently she'd been acting like a madwoman. It wasn't our fault that things weren't good with her husband. And the neighbors said:

"We're used to her scandals. We know the whole repertoire. We take no notice of her any longer. There's never any end to their quarreling."

And then there were two days left. She told us again: "Leave!"

We told the children to go to Aunty Lida after school, and we set out to look for an apartment. We went on looking until midnight. Nothing at all. I almost went mad.

In the morning I went to the migration center again. I went into the office. I was seen by the same man, the one who saw

me before. There was a secretary sitting beside him, or a col-
league, I don't know. He asked:

"What did you want? What's your question?"

I was so anxious I was shaking all over. I said to him:

"You see, I was here to see you before, and I'd like to know,
if someone with children is left out on the street in winter in
Russia, what do they do about it?"

"Where did you come from?"

"From Turkmenia."

"And why did you come to our town? The whole place is
already crammed with immigrants."

"Then won't you tell me where isn't crammed?"

"Everywhere's crammed, the whole of Russia's crammed!
What did you come to Russia for? Go back home!"

"We have a certificate from the Russian embassy that says
I'm a Russian citizen and so are my children. It was for their
sake that I came here to Russia. Where we come from in
Turkmenia there's a lot of drug addiction, and it's very bad
there now."

"And you think things are good in Russia, do you? There's
nothing good here. There's nothing we can do to help you,
go back home."

"I've already deregistered there, and I'm not going to go
back. In Turkmenia my children will be nobody, they only
speak Russian."

While he was talking to someone on the telephone, I turned
to that secretary, I cried and said:

"You know, we've already been in Russia for a year and a half. We live in other people's apartments, we don't even have the money to buy a room in a communal apartment. Now I'm quite literally out on the street, a tramp with children. I'd like to know, if someone with children ends up out on the street in the Russian state, what do they do about it? Put them in a hostel or at least a broken-down ruin, do they give them anything at all? Here, look at my documents, I'm a Russian citizen too!" And I took out all my documents.

She looked at everything and said:

"You have all the documents, but that's not the point. Right now no one will do anything for you, they won't give you a room in a hostel or anything at all."

"How can that be? It's winter, and my children will die!"

"I don't know, it doesn't depend on me. Go to an agency that rents out apartments. Perhaps they have something for money."

"I've been round all the agencies in the town in the last year and a half. It's always the same answer: We don't take non-Russians, and especially not with children."

Just then the boss put down the phone and turned to me:

"What were you thinking when you came to Russia? People come here to their relatives or friends, but who did you come to?"

I didn't want to talk about that subject, because it was our relatives' fault that we'd ended up on the street. I answered:

"We didn't come to anyone, we came on our own."

He said:

"Then go back!"

"But isn't there anywhere we can stay in Russia?"

"Go to Siberia, to the taiga, and live there with the bears!" he answered.

"All right, thank you," I said, and I went out into the street. And I thought: Then why did they set up this useless migration center, if they can't do anything there? And they pay them wages too—what for? So that they can send illiterate people like me off to the bears, is that it? I can live anywhere at all, I've survived the desert, I spent all night in the forest until morning—I didn't die. And now they send me off to the bears. I can live with the bears too! But the point is: Why make the children suffer, what for? That's the way it is! The state is like an X-ray machine, it looks right through me. It looks straight through me and doesn't even notice me.

And so I walked around the town and I said to myself:

Are we really going to be left out on the street today?

I went to the people I knew at the market.

"I need an apartment urgently," I said. "We've literally been left out on the street."

They were alarmed and they asked:

"But where are the children?"

"In school."

They all started offering us places at once. One woman said:

"Come to us! Until you find an apartment, you can live with me. Of course, my son and I only have one room. We'll sleep on the floor, or you can, we'll fit in somehow. Come, all right? Here's the address, take it."

Another woman said:

"Come stay with us, my children will be glad."

I answered:

"There are five of you, and four of us, no, no, thank you!"

"But where will you go? You'd better come, all right? Here's the address."

There was a woman standing nearby. She said:

"Listen, there's an empty apartment in our building, the owner's still a young man, forty years old, he's divorced, he mostly lives with his father in the country."

"But how can we find him?"

"I see him sometimes."

"Sometimes is no good to me, I need him right now!"

"I understand, but how can I find him right now? I can't do it until tomorrow."

"All right, we'll hold on until tomorrow. We'll stay with friends until then. When you find him, tell me, please. If he complains because of the children, tell him that they aren't noisy and they're at school the whole day."

"All right, tomorrow I'll go to the collective farm market, he sometimes goes there, or I'll call into the grocery store over that way, he used to work there as a porter. If they haven't sacked him for drinking yet, we'll arrange things tomorrow. Just don't you be upset, everything will be fine."

* * *

We spent the night with friends. In the morning the children went to school, and we went to the market. I found the woman there and I asked:

"Well, did you see the owner of that apartment?"

"I did, I agreed with him that you'd stay at his place for a long time. I explained that you'd pay the money on time, but how much and for what, you can agree between yourselves."

"Of course we'll pay the money on time!" I said happily.

"Then go, he's waiting for you at the apartment. You can work out all the details with him there."

My husband and I went to agree to terms. We knocked at the door. It was broken. We went into the apartment—ugh! I'd never seen anything so horrible.

In the corridor a cobweb stuck right to my face. Two rooms were full of rubbish, and there was all sorts of lumber lying around everywhere. A broken divan, broken guitars, cobwebs hanging everywhere. I went into the kitchen—a heap of dirty dishes was standing in the sink. I saw the refrigerator and I thought: Strange, do they make black refrigerators, then? But that refrigerator was covered with black mold. I opened it and almost fell down. The owner of the flat, Yura, said:

"It works, it works."

I went into the bathroom and saw a yellow bath. It was horrible, I'd never seen anything like it before. I can't even tell you about the toilet. The whole apartment smelled of urine anyway.

We agreed terms with the owner. From his eyes alone you could see he was an alcoholic. But what else could we do. We had to!

"So this is my apartment," he said. "You just tidy things up a little bit, and everything will be fine!"

And suddenly I noticed that it was even colder in the apartment than outside. It turned out that none of the windows in the kitchen or any of the rooms had any frames or glass in them. There was a terrible draft, after all it was November.

We walked around the rooms, and everywhere dust rose into the air from under our feet. And that alcoholic also announced:

"If you need the flat, first pay off the ten months of rent that I owe. Agreed?"

That was all we needed! But we had to pay his debts at the savings bank. I paid and brought back the receipt.

Straightaway my husband went to the market, made some frames, put them in, and put glass in them. Then it was a little warmer in the apartment. The same day we moved away from Ravil and Galya to the new place, the alcoholic's apartment. The children still went to the same school, although it was quite far now, but they were used to it, and so I didn't move them. What for? They'd only be picked on again, as new boys. Let them stay in a school they liked.

As always, I started cleaning up the new place. The black refrigerator took me five days, and I was cleaning the bath for ten whole days. If you only knew! While I was cleaning that rust, all the skin came off my hands. I must have bought all the household chemicals in the town to clean off that filth. The things I did! And clearing up the chaos in the apartment and cleaning everything took me about twenty days.

We began living there. The owner of the flat came eight times in a single week, asking for money: either two hundred or a hundred fifty or a hundred or fifty. I said to him:

"We've just paid the rent you owed. I don't print money, we work hard to get it!"

He went away. Then he came back again to beg.

Our trading was coming along slowly.

We were living with only a temporary registration. You could say we were trading illegally. At the market I asked the traders I knew and the customers who were regular if anyone had a grandfather or grandmother in the country who needed money. But they were all afraid when anyone mentioned registration. They avoided answering. But I pestered everyone: "Register us, register us!"

And then I asked a woman who had bought from me several times, sometimes a shirt, sometimes a pair of shoes:

"Excuse me, please, can I ask you something?"

"Yes, of course."

"I don't have any money to buy an apartment and register, I work illegally, with just a temporary registration. That registration will end soon. Couldn't you register me where you live? I'll sign all the documents to say I don't have any claims on your apartment."

See what I'd come to in my despair!

She answered:

"I understand everything. But I live in the region, not the town, I have to find out if our rural council will agree or not."

Anyway, Valya (that was her name) promised to help us.

Two days later she came and said that she would register us. I almost went mad, I was so happy. I asked her to wait and dashed home from the market as fast as I could. I grabbed two hundred dollars and ran back, and meanwhile Ikram was trading for me. I ran up to our booth, where Valya was waiting, and gave her the money. She said:

"No, there's no need, I'll register you without it."

"Take it, take it, you have children too, you can use it!"

She took the money and went away. And I never saw her again.

Then I went to Moscow again to buy goods at the Cherkizovo market. I bought a ticket. I'd prepared everything for the children at home. I took all the money, I didn't even leave any for bread. I thought my husband would sell something at the market while I was away—there would be money, there would be bread.

We reached the Cherkizovo market. I got out of the bus like all the traders and went to buy goods. I spent all the money on goods, I was going back to the bus, and I stopped in front of a stall to ask: "How much are the blouses?" That was all. But the buggy with the things was standing behind me. While I was looking at those blouses, they stole my bag. I turned round and my bag was gone, vanished into thin air. I was upset, I ran this way and that through the crowd. But how could I find the bag now? It was gone, stolen!

I had an empty buggy, no money . . . I walked to the bus, completely exhausted. The driver asked:

"Where are your goods?"

"They stole my goods."

"You have to be careful here, or you'll be left with nothing."

I was in torment in the bus: Why had I stopped by the blouses? I wouldn't have bought any anyway, and because of those blouses they'd stolen all my goods, fifty-two hundred rubles' worth. While we were going back, I didn't eat anything on the way—I had no money. I thought: Never mind, I'll eat at home.

I got home, I explained to my husband that they'd stolen my bag. He reassured me, but I could see he was very upset. Then he told me he hadn't sold anything the whole day, there was no trading. And so we were left without bread. As if on purpose the children kept asking for bread until eleven o'clock in the evening. I cooked something for them, but they kept demanding bread, nothing else. When there was white bread and black bread lying in the bread bin, they didn't eat it—but now there was no bread, it was bread they wanted.

We survived somehow until the morning. Early in the morning we got up to go to the market and trade. Suddenly there was a ring at the door. We opened it and saw the landlord had come to ask us to lend him money.

We tried to explain the situation to him—he didn't believe us:

"Then borrow it from someone," he said.

I answered:

"We haven't had any bread for ourselves or the children since yesterday, and I'm not in the habit of asking anybody for money."

He kept on:

"Give me at least five roubles."

"If I had five roubles," I said, "I'd have bought bread for the children already. You stop bothering us, you won't get anything. When you come for the monthly rent on the first of the month, that's when I'll give you money. You managed to live without us before, carry on living like that. In the other place it was the relatives always saying 'give, give' and now it's you!"

He went away, and we went off to the market. I prayed to God to let us sell at least something, because one son had stayed at home without anything to eat, and the other had gone to school, they would feed him for free there.

Then when I sold something I ran to the shop straightaway, bought some food, and hurried back to the apartment. I fed my son and went back to the market. At the market some people had heard I had no money left and my bag had been stolen in Moscow. One of the people I'd traveled with the day before had told them. The women came up to me and said:

"Do you have any money? If you need some, you just say, all right?"

"All day yesterday and until ten o'clock today the children were hungry and so were we, there was nothing to eat at home."

"Ah, you fool, somebody must have hit you on the head with a brick, why did you leave the children hungry? You should have asked us for money for bread! How could you do that?"

"I never ask anyone for anything. Look, I've just sold some goods, and now I'll buy bread. If you borrow money, you have to be able to pay it back. So I never ask anyone for money. Thank you for coming to support me!"

"Don't despair, we've been through all that, they stole our bags and pinched our money. It's all happened to us. Money's not so important, you can earn it. Just as long as you have your health."

After my friend left I noticed that another woman, also a trader—her booth was about three meters from ours—was standing there calling me names:

"Little bitch, swine, louse! Look at that, she's brought the same goods as I have. What a louse!"

I didn't say anything. But she went on:

"Stupid cow! Just watch, I'll sell everything below cost, and she can go bankrupt. The illiterate swine, bitch, louse!"

I didn't say anything. She went on calling me names for an hour. I didn't know what to do. By the way, she had spoken with me before, but there were only a few phrases in her vocabulary: "plain ignorance, idiocy." Everyone around her was stupid and illiterate, but she was a doctor, she'd graduated from a college and an academy. She always told everyone that she was very well educated, because she'd graduated from a medical academy, which wasn't true. And now she was standing in her trading booth and calling me names nonstop.

If only you knew the state I was in: yesterday they'd stolen my bag, when I got back my children were hungry and there was no money at home, and first thing in the morning the landlord had appeared and asked to borrow money, and here at the market I was being called all sorts of names. I had no more strength left. I couldn't stand it anymore. I went across to her and I said:

"Excuse me, Zoya Afanasievna, why are you calling me a bitch?"

"You've no right to go bringing in the same goods as me!"

"So are you saying this is your own private market?"

"Don't bring in my goods!"

"And please don't you call me a bitch!"

I couldn't bear those insults anymore. It was like something inside me snapped. I burst into tears, fell on my knees. Put my arms round her boots, pressed my forehead against them, and begged her:

"Please don't call me names!"

She pushed me away with her foot and walked off, swearing, to her second trading spot, and went on calling me names there. They helped me get up and told me:

"Calm down! You fool, why did you go down on your knees, she's not worth it!"

I was still crying:

"But why does she call me names?"

"In cases like that what we say round here is: 'Go . . . yourself.'"

"I don't know the translation of that word."

"You just tell her without any translation."

I went back to my place. I could hear her standing at her second spot, still doing it:

". . . stupid ignorant idiots."

"Don't call me names," and I fell down on the snow. I don't remember what happened after that. My legs wouldn't move, I lost consciousness.

When I came round, I saw a few women beside me. Someone brought me medicines, someone poured me tea. One elderly woman went over to Zoya Afanasievna and said:

"Zoya, you're a doctor, help her."

Then she came across to me and checked my pulse:

"A fit of nerves, it will pass in a moment. Bibish, apparently they stole your bag yesterday, I didn't know about that, I'm sorry," and she turned away.

I didn't have enough strength left to answer her. I lay there without saying anything, that was all. Then they saw me home, so that I wouldn't fall again. There was nobody at home. I was sobbing so hard! Why have I been so humiliated, I thought, what for? I wanted to die.

The next day I got up early. It was Ikram's birthday. Naturally, I wished him happy birthday. We had breakfast and went to the market. We went up to our trading booth, and when I saw it, I almost fainted. Someone had slashed it to pieces. There wasn't a single part left whole. Everybody looked at us, at our reaction. We stood there without saying anything, I just cried, that was all. My husband said:

"Well, that's a big present for my birthday!"

We spent from the morning until nine in the evening sticking the pieces together with sticky tape. All the people were amazed that we worked in silence and didn't try to find out who was to blame. But we said: "God is the judge," and that was all.

Zoya came up to us and said:

"Stupid, ignorant idiots, it wasn't me!"

"We didn't say anything to you."

"It was probably drunken hooligans."

"Perhaps."

After that happened, Zoya probably realized that she could taunt me. I didn't know how to answer her back, and my husband kept quiet too, he didn't defend me. From that day she began attacking me.

Every morning we came to the market and laid out our things. Zoya came over to our booth with her hands on her hips and examined our goods. Since she was trading not far away, she used to come every half hour and get on our nerves. When her trade went badly, she blamed me. She said:

"We don't need their hordes here!"

The women traders I knew at the market told me:

"If I was in your place, Bibish, I'd tear her to pieces!"

Another said:

"Why didn't your husband defend you? If mine was here, he'd have beaten that Zoya to a pulp."

And they said:

"She won't leave you alone now, she'll keep on pressing you. You shouldn't have gone down on your knees in front of her."

Zoya really did carry on with her insults. She muttered and swore and drove our customers away.

I remembered what my grandmother Niyazdjan had told me: If they beat you on one cheek, offer them the other. I hadn't understood those words before. But now I realized what they meant. Of course, all this affected me. I became irritable, I accused my husband of not defending me.

One day Ikram came home a little bit drunk. At that moment I was cooking soup for supper. I laid the table, poured soup for the children and myself. But I didn't take any notice of my husband. I said to the children:

"If you drink like him, you'll be like the winos."

The children ate their soup without saying anything.

I think I overdid it. Ikram stood up and moved close to me:

"All right, say that again, what you just said. What are you teaching the children? Want them to have no respect for me, do you?"

I told him what was tormenting me.

"Why didn't you stand up for me? If you'd supported me, I wouldn't have gone down on my knees!"

"I'm a man, I'm not going to get involved in women's business. If I start sorting her out, I won't be able to answer for myself. Do you want them to put me in jail?"

"No!"

"Then why do you whine every day?"

He gave a terrible shout, then he grabbed my plate of soup and poured it over my head. I kept quiet, I didn't say anything else. He grabbed the back of a chair and hit me with it. The chair shattered into pieces. The children were frightened, and they started shouting too:

"Dad, don't! Dad, don't!"

But he threw their plates of soup against the wall.

The children's hearts almost leapt out of their mouths. Because we'd never, ever seen him in such a state! He broke four plates and two chairs. It was a good thing the television wasn't near, or he'd have broken that too.

I was bleeding from my mouth and my nose. The children ran to look for cotton wool and bandages. But he shouted:

"Sit down! That's what she deserves, she shouldn't have made a spectacle of herself at the market! Why did you go down on your knees, eh?" and he started beating me round the head with his fists.

Then he stopped and demanded his documents. And he carried on abusing me:

"What kind of person are you? You gave away two hundred dollars to a woman you didn't know, you got distracted at the market in Moscow and they stole your bag, you can't deal with that Zoya!"

I could see he was really sick of everything, that was why he hit me, he couldn't bear it any longer.

He started looking for his documents, he wandered round the apartment and rifled through everything. I realized this was something serious, and I hid his documents quickly.

He was tired, exhausted. He lay down on the bed and fell asleep like that with his clothes and his shoes on.

In the morning I got up and looked, and there were bruises on my hands and face. There was a soup stain on the wall. I didn't know where to put myself. Look, I thought, I've spoiled everything at home as well. I walked around like a robot, I did everything mechanically.

Several days went by like that. I started thinking about death again, about the best way to die. Should I open my veins? Then I thought: If I die like that, there'll be no memory left of me, no one will even remember me! Before I die, I'll bring people at least a little bit of joy, I'll dance real eastern dances for them! After all, here it's mostly specially trained girls who dance, but I'm from the East.

I wrote a letter to Moscow, to the television. I told them about myself. Surely, I thought, they'll be interested in my story! What if they ask me to come, and then perhaps my whole life will change . . . After all, how do things happen in real life? A person's success is determined by the fuss someone else stirs up around them. I wrote to the program *Field of Miracles* and to *The Big Wash* and to *My Family*. And, like a fool, I waited for an answer. One day I asked a girlfriend of mine:

"Do you know anybody, or do any of your friends know anybody who's been on television even once?"

She laughed:

"It's hopeless. My own mother-in-law wrote to them for ten years."

"And what happened?"
"Nothing. In the end she died."

All the same, the people in television are strange: If some terrorist commits an act of terror, they start showing it and talking about it . . . as if nothing else in the world existed! But here was someone who only wanted to make people happy for three minutes, to offer them her eastern art (and not a bomb!). But that's not possible. How lucky those rotten terrorists are: they show them on television day and night, eating, pissing, studying, and finally committing an act of terror!

I was foolish to hope, to think that my art would help me. It was pointless expecting anything to happen. It made me lose heart. I stopped taking care of myself, or the children, or my husband, I didn't clean the apartment. I lived like a homeless vagrant. I wore some kind of tattered old fluffy headscarves . . .

The children started crying and saying:

"Mom, don't walk around like that. They'll call us tramps. They won't leave us alone as it is. We have enough problems without you."

It was true, because the day before my younger son had come in from the yard all covered in spit, the children had just taken him and spat on him from his head to his feet!

My husband couldn't stand any more, he said:

"You've lost all sense of shame. I understand everything—things are hard for us, with no home of our own . . . But at least wash yourself, comb your hair, dress decently!"

At first I wouldn't listen to anyone. I thought God had made my life out of one long streak of bad luck. But then I gradually calmed down. I took myself in hand. And then I began to write a book about my life. Simply to unburden my soul. And so that some memory of me would be left for my children and grandchildren.

At the new apartment, the alcoholic Yura's place, we got to know the neighbors again.

They started inviting us, sometimes to wakes, sometimes to birthdays. They were very good people. Though they were mostly elderly. Recently two of them had been in the hospital, I visited them by turns, they were so pleased. And when one of them was discharged from the hospital, we became even closer.

One old woman who lived not far from us was fond of my children and me. She invited me to her place for Christmas. A lot of people were there, and our neighbor Vera was one of them. That evening we got to know each other better. She said:

"Bibish, if you have any problems or difficulties, come to me. I'll do everything I can to help you!"

A few days went by, the thirteenth of January arrived, and I invited my neighbors to my birthday, and to celebrate the old New Year at the same time. All the neighbors came. And Vera came as well. Straightaway she took my children to her place, so they could play games on the computer, and then came back to us.

We celebrated my birthday, everything was fine. The neighbors said:

"Your landlord made such a mess of this apartment! We thought it was impossible to live here, but Bibish has tidied everything up, there are plants growing here, even lemon trees!"

Yes, in the apartment I really did have twenty pots with different plants and two lemon trees. The landlord once opened the door of our room and said:

"I thought I'd walked into a botanical garden!"

Where I got the plants from is another interesting story.

The Story of Where My Plants Came From

When I was still living with Galya's neighbor, I used to go to the grocery store with a glass jar for the unbottled milk. The shop assistant always used to scold me:

"Don't come with a glass jar, what if it breaks! Bring a milk can for the milk."

I started looking for a can for the milk. One day I saw a woman sitting on the sidewalk and selling old things: plates, spoons, forks. Suddenly I noticed there was a milk can there as well. Straightaway I went up to her and asked:

"Are you selling the milk can?"

"Yes, yes, of course, take it!"

"How much?"

"Only fifteen roubles."

"Oh, how cheap! But where's its lid?"

"There isn't a lid."

"Then how am I going to carry the milk?"

"Well, when you go for the milk, take the lid off the kettle and put it on the can!"

"But does the lid from a kettle fit a milk can?"

"Of course!"

"If you only knew how hard I've looked for this can! They're always scolding me for my glass jar."

"Surely there ought to be milk cans in the shops? There must be . . ."

"There are some in the shops, but they're expensive, and I'd like something a bit cheaper, we're newcomers, you know—we haven't got enough money for everything we need . . ."

"Where did you come from?" she asked.

"From Central Asia."

"I'm from there too!"

I was surprised and I asked:

"How do you mean?"

She answered:

"I'm Russian, but I was born in Uzbekistan. My parents moved to Central Asia earlier. So I was born there, in

Uzbekistan. And I married my Russian husband there. Then we moved to Turkmenia and lived there until we retired."

"But why are you selling your things?"

"We moved here to Russia ten years ago, our daughter was studying in Leningrad. She got married there. Now she wants us to go. We've sold our apartment, our daughter has bought us two rooms in Petersburg. She has everything there, so that's why I'm selling my old junk. Oh, why didn't we meet sooner? What a pity we're going away! Wait, let's go to our place, you can take everything you need! I'll just give it to you, we're from the same parts, after all." Ikram and I went to her apartment. Her husband was packing their things. That was how we got to know Uncle Fedya. He was born in Tambov, but he'd lived all his life in Central Asia. He gave us the twenty plants and the two lemon trees. And a bed as well, three chairs, felt boots, cushions, curtains, and a writing desk.

As they were saying good-bye to us, they said:

"When you water the plants, remember us: 'Thanks to Zhanna Petrovna and Uncle Fedya, we have a botanical garden now.'" So now the plants shift from apartment to apartment with us. My husband looks after them.

Finally I decided to go to the police to find out if I was entitled to a Russian passport or not. Just how did anyone get a passport here? After all, I had all the documents. People advised me:

"At the police station you have to talk clearly and be brief."

So I went to the passport office. I waited my turn in a long line and went in to the boss. She asked:

"What did you want? I'm listening."

"I want to have a passport."

She was surprised and asked:

"What's that you say?"

"I want a passport."

"And is that all you want?" she asked rudely.

I took offense and didn't say anything. She reached out her hand:

"Give me your documents! Your documents please!"

I gave her everything straightaway. She looked at my papers and started saying something. She talked and talked and at the end I heard:

"And then we'll give you a passport!"

That was the only phrase I remembered. For a year and a half I went round lots of passport offices, and in every district they explained things to me differently. Perhaps I didn't understand them very well because I didn't know the language? In some places they even said: "Come back with an interpreter!" And then Vera finally explained to me that I had to buy a house or an apartment, then I'd have a permanent registration and I could get a Russian passport.

I said I didn't have enough money to buy a place to live. She advised me:

"Houses are cheaper in country districts. Buy the newspaper *From Hands to Hands,* there's absolutely everything in it! You can find something to suit your pocket."

I bought that newspaper and began phoning people. Sixty kilometers from the town, in a rural area, I found a place to live—for seven hundred American dollars. I went there. I agreed terms with the owner and in a week they registered all my documents. And we paid the money straightaway.

We went to the local passport office, they checked all my documents there and said: "Your passport will be ready in a week, come back in a week!"

We went to pick up my passport. I went into the boss's office and she told me:

"Go over to that little window, they'll give you your passport."

I went to the little window and they told me:

"Check your first name, family name, and patronymic and the dates."

"Everything's all right!"

"Sign here!"

I signed. I had a new Russian passport! I opened it and looked: the date of issue was the thirteenth of February. Amazing! Because in my old Turkmenian passport the date of issue was the thirteenth of November. My birthday is the thirteenth of January. My first son was born on the thirteenth of April. My second was born on the thirteenth of May. Really! You couldn't make it up!

I took my passport and went running to the car. We set off to the rural council to register. When we'd gone about twenty kilometers I shouted:

"Oh, I forgot!"

"What did you forget?"

"I left the children's birth certificates in the passport office. What do you think, will they give them back to me?"

"Of course, just tell them you forgot them."

"I was so nervous!"

We went back to the passport office, straight to the boss. She understood everything and said:

"Here are your children's certificates."

"I was nervous because I was so happy: I suffered for a year and a half over that passport! Now my suffering is over, thank you very much, good-bye!"

We went home and celebrated my new passport with the neighbors. They just gasped at the number thirteen. The number thirteen was written everywhere.

Now I am calm.

I thanked Vera for supporting me and helping me. I went to the Sapphire shop and bought some silver earrings—I couldn't afford gold ones—and gave them to her as a keepsake.

But my calm life didn't last long. One day there was a ring at the door. I opened it. There was our landlord standing there. He could barely stay on his feet.

I asked:

"What is it, have you come to ask for money again?"

"No, I want to go to the toilet, my stomach's not feeling good."

"Yes, of course, I think you should drink less!"

He went through into the room and right there in front of my eyes he dumped in his pants and then fell on the floor. I barely managed to lift him up and lead him into the bathroom. If you only knew how the apartment stank! I couldn't stand it, I went out onto the balcony. The landlord washed himself a bit and lay down on the divan.

I looked, and the whole room, the kitchen, and the bathroom were covered in filth. What could I do? I had to clean up. We lived there, after all. I found some rubber gloves and got a bucket of water. I tied a headscarf round my face and left just my eyes. I was afraid I'd be sick.

When I'd cleaned it all up, I went over to Yura:

"You ought to be ashamed of yourself. You're forty years old, not forty days, you shouldn't be dumping in your pants!"

He didn't even react at all. Later he came round and left. And soon he went away to his relatives in the country.

A month later there was another ring at the door. I opened it and there were two people standing there: a man and a woman.

"We're from the Housing Committee, can we come in?"

"Please do." And I was thinking: What do they want, we pay the rent and all the utility bills on time. "What's happened?"

"Your landlord Yura has died. You have to vacate the apartment immediately."

"What do you mean, died? He's so young." I was dumbfounded, it was such a surprise.

"He drank a lot, and so he died. We know that you're his tenants. But now we have to seal up the premises."

I was completely flabbergasted.

"Wait," I said, "he has a son, you know. Perhaps we can agree terms with him."

"That won't work. The son isn't registered here, the apartment goes to the state. Look for somewhere to live quickly. In a week we'll come and seal everything up here."

"But you can't do that! It's winter, after all, what will I do with my children?"

"That's your problem. Look for an apartment."

I ran round the neighbors, I put up a notice at the market, I phoned an agency. It was useless. What a terrible life I had! That's what it means to be born on the thirteenth.

A week later the people from the Housing Committee came again.

"I haven't found anything yet."

"That's no concern of ours."

"Tell me, do you have children?"

"Yes."

"Then wait at least one more day," I begged them.

They agreed. They gave me another day. But what was I hoping for? What guarantee was there that I'd find an apartment in that day? We went to bed in a terrible state. In the morning there was a ring at the door. One of our neighbors was standing there.

"I felt so sorry for you," she said, "every day I went walking round the entrances in our building, looking for an apartment. You've lived here for more than a year, after all. We've got used to you, it will be a shame if you leave. And I found an apartment on the fifth floor, the owner lives with her aunt."

I was so happy I smothered her with kisses and said to myself: God did hear my prayer after all!

And that very day we moved to the other apartment. Just at that time I was expecting visitors from America. It was a good thing they didn't see me running around looking for a place to live, like some kind of vagrant!

You are probably surprised: Why would she have visitors from America?

I'll tell you now. And this story about the Americans will be the last in my book: the period of bad luck seems to be over and a good period has begun. But that's another book already.

Well then, one day I got to know Linda at the neighbors' place. She'd come from America, from the city of Seattle. She worked in Russia, teaching children and grown-ups English.

I didn't have a word of English and she didn't have a word of Russian either. But we understood each other somehow. Sometimes an interpreter helped us to talk. She was an extraordinary person too, by the way. Would an ordinary person come from America to the Russian provinces in order to make people's life there better? As well as being a teacher, Linda's an ordained priest. She's a volunteer who helps at-risk children and women. And no one forces her to do it, by the way. That's just the kind of person she is, she needs to do it.

It turned out that Linda lived in our building. And our building, as you've probably guessed, is the simplest possible old five-story block. The entrances are smelly and not always clean.

We started meeting each other. In America, Linda has two sons, two daughters-in-law, and seven grandchildren! Although the second daughter-in-law appeared only recently.

For the first time I felt that someone was interested in my life, that someone wanted to help the children and me. Linda started teaching my children English, for free of course. And she helped us with money too.

When she came to visit us, I treated her to bread cakes and pilaf—our eastern food. One day we invited all the staff of the mission where she works, twenty-five people, to visit us. We sat and ate pilaf, talked, and laughed. I told them about our eastern culture. I showed them a few dances. They liked them a lot. They were surprised that no one here was interested in my art.

It didn't bother Linda at all that I was poorly dressed or that we lived in an apartment where the wallpaper was tattered and the floor was horrible (what else could it be like in a place that belonged to an alcoholic!). She raised my spirits. Once she said that my family was her family too.

That winter Linda had a birthday. I wondered what could I give her, how could I thank her? I asked the interpreter. She laughed:

"What could you surprise them with? They have everything!" And then she said: "Listen, you dance . . . Record that on a tape and give it to Linda. That will be a really unusual present!"

Right, I thought, good. And so my art was useful after all. I bought some shiny material. Ikram sewed me a costume with his own hands. I began looking for suitable music. I couldn't find any anywhere. Then I ran to the collective farm market, the young men there are Azerbaijanis. "Help me out," I said, I told them this and that. The next day they brought five cassettes, so I was able to choose. The children made me headdresses out of cardboard for the different dances: I was going to do an Uzbek dance, and one from Khorezm, and a Turkish one, and an Iranian one (after all, I have Iranian blood in my veins too), and an Arabian one, and an Afghan one. And

I'd also made up a dance dedicated to all mothers so that I could dance it especially for Linda. The Americans brought costume jewelery they rented.

Now I had to find a hall. After all, I didn't know anyone in the cultural administration. Renting a hall was expensive. I didn't have any money to spare. I thought and thought and decided to ask the school my children went to. They decided to help me out straightaway. Only they said: "We don't have any sound equipment, and the hall is in terrible condition, we didn't manage to do any repairs in the summer."

But that was no disaster! I had so much enthusiasm. For two days I washed the floors and wiped off the dust. Ikram mended sixty-two chairs with his own hands and fixed the benches. We brought in plants in pots from the director's office, the other offices, and our neighbors to decorate the hall. Everything was ready for my first solo concert, dedicated to Linda.

So that the hall wouldn't be half-empty, we decided to invite our traders from the market as well. No one at the market believed it. They thought I was making things up. They were all used to looking at me as some kind of vagrant. And it's true that my appearance didn't match my invitation. And at the market no one knew that I not only had secondary specialized education, but higher education too. They thought I was some kind of primitive. But by the way, an airship is primitive too, but it flies!

Some of them weren't shy about it, they said straight out:

"Surely you're not going to dance! What a joke! When did you become a dancer?"

They whispered behind my back as well:

"What an ignorant Chukcha! She can't even speak Russian properly!"

And what of it? As it happens, God made the Chukchas too. And if you'd like to know, the most inoffensive people live in "Chukchistan."

But I have a bad habit: I tell all my joys and sorrows to everyone straightaway. At the market, when they learned I was friends with Americans, they got really angry:

"Would you ever, see how lucky the black faces are!"

They laughed and gossiped. It turns out people are all alike: it's the same here as in my native kishlak.

Then the day of the concert arrived. About two hundred people gathered. And my friend Theodore Walls was there, an anthropologist from Detroit, he was my patron as well. I danced from the heart. Afterward there was applause and flowers. People came up to me and thanked me. And Linda sat there and cried. At the end of the dance dedicated to all mothers, I took off my headdress and put it on her head. Everything went very well.

I express my thoughts without any words—in the dances that I make up. Without speaking, but clearly! The dances turn out most unusual when I'm suffering or, just the opposite, when I'm happy about something.

After that concert people in the town began to know me a little. They began inviting me to dance for money at parties, in houses of culture. But even so it is very hard to break through and realize my potential. I'll never be another Tamara Hanum. The times aren't right.

And several months later, Linda's younger son John came with his bride, Magenta, and lived with us. In the morning my children woke up and said: "Mom, do we really have American guests, sleeping in the same apartment as us, we just can't believe it." It really was quite fantastic!

They both know about art and music and they write poems. I showed them one of my dances. They liked it a lot, they said the movements were beautiful and it was very expressive. They asked why I didn't dance. I didn't say anything, I couldn't tell them that no one here was interested.

I also told them that in my free time I was writing an autobiographical book that was called "A Cry from the Heart" (that was what the book you are reading was called at first). They were interested and asked me to let them take a photocopy. They said: "Would you like us to take it to America, translate it into English, and publish it?"

An unexpected suggestion like that really set my head spinning.

On the thirteenth of January we celebrated my birthday together, then soon after that they went away and took my book and the cassette of my dances with them. They were on their honeymoon traveling in Europe, through Holland, Denmark, France, and then they were in Ireland. And so you could say my art has been everywhere in the world!

It seemed to me that I'd been almost as low as I could get, and God had sent these people to me.

So that was how more and more bright times began appearing in my life. Now I hope for the best.

And I want to finish the book with a letter to my father. I tried to find the right words for it for a long time, but I just couldn't. Finally I've managed to write it.

A LETTER OF REPENTANCE TO MY FATHER

Hello, my dear dad! Here I am at last writing you a letter. Perhaps you've been waiting for me to do it for a long, long time. My life lies like a stone on your heart. Dad, it's good that God has taken pity on me and now I can apologize to you. I couldn't find the words for a long time. I wasn't really in touch with myself. But this is what happened today: When I was standing in our market, a real storm began to blow. The sky turned black, a wild wind sprang up, the trees swayed, the roofs were torn off several houses (they showed it on the television later!). It started tearing the tarpaulins off the trading booths as well. And at that inappropriate moment I suddenly realized what I had to write. I found a pencil, but I didn't have any paper! I went dashing to a trader nearby who was packing up his goods and getting ready to leave. I shouted:

"Give me some paper!"

He said:

"What do you want paper for now? There's a hurricane starting!"

"I have to write a letter to my father!"

"Were you waiting specially for a hurricane to start to do that? Will cardboard do?"

"Yes, as long as I can write on it!"

I ran to my place and wrote down on that piece of cardboard the most important thing I wanted to say. And the boards that hold together the top of the booth were tumbling down on me. Now I'm continuing the letter at home.

My grandmother Niyazdjan told me how I was born. The women in our kishlak used to have their children at home, they didn't go to the hospital. A midwife used to come to help them give birth. And all the relatives and friends would be there in the house. In our parts women give birth standing, leaning on a long stick like a pole. It's easier to push like that. And so my mother was leaning on this pole and she squatted down, she was just about to give birth! My grandmother called you:

"Nizom, the birth's starting, come quickly!"

You had to help, bring some warm water and something else as well.

But at that moment you were writing a plan for a lesson and you kept saying:

"I'll come after I finish this, I'll come in a moment."

My grandmother said:

"Son, the child can't wait, come quickly!"

Before you could even touch me, I just popped out and tumbled on to the old kurpachka. *I was born very quickly.*

Later, when I started writing stories in the sixth grade, Mom used to remember that I was born when you were writing your lesson plan.

I was restless from when I was little. I was always trying to swim against the current. I wanted to be an artist, not an ordinary one but one with a capital letter. I wanted to "discover America" in the kishlak. But America was discovered by poor Christopher Columbus, who suffered torments for his ideas and died a pauper!

I know all the things I did were outrageous for our kishlak. And I didn't think about you, or my brothers and sisters. I thought only about myself. And in the end I ran away to Leningrad. But no one knew about that disgrace, because when they asked you, you said: "She's away studying."

Dad, I remember when I was six or seven, you sat me on the frame of your bicycle and we went to Khiva. Probably to do some shopping. It was spring, nice and warm, the fruit trees were in blossom. We were riding past our lake and you were singing a song, you always hum it, even now. It had these words in it: "If a rose grows in a nightingale's cage, he will think it a dry briar!"

I remember that song of yours, and it seems to me that deep in your heart you must have understood the things I did.

In the summer you always used to lay in fuel for the winter. You scraped the dung out of the cowshed, then mixed it with kerosene that you got from the tractor drivers and made flat cakes by hand.

One morning I found you doing this heavy work. I took a broom and started sprinkling the yard with water in order to sweep it. When I was very close to you the water accidentally got onto your sweaty back. You got angry and threw the spade you were using to mix the dung at me. The spade hit my leg. It hurt a lot. Then your anger cooled and you came over to me, but at that moment I hated you! I didn't understand then that you were messing around with manure for our sake, so that we wouldn't be cold and ill in winter.

And when in one year my two brothers and my sister all died one after another, you almost went out of your mind, you wanted to go away with the whole family to the Far East. But you didn't go, there wasn't enough money. It's probably good that you didn't go, because just at that time there was a powerful earthquake in the Far East and many people were killed.

When Mom was very angry with me, she used to say: "It would be better if you had never been born!" But now I don't regret that I was born, although my life is very difficult. But then after all, for grandmother Niyazdjan and for you life was hard too. For you books were the most important things in life. Perhaps it will make you happy to know that I have been able to write this book.

Forgive me, I know some pages will be hard for you to read. And forgive me for the pain I have caused you, my dear dad, if you can, forgive me!

Your daughter Hadjar

2987/west
1/10/09